BRIEF TYPING

SECOND EDITION
REVISED

By

GEORGE L. HOSSFIELD

and

JULIUS NELSON

THE H. M. ROWE COMPANY

BALTIMORE   CHICAGO

INDEX

Revised 1977, 1966 © **The H. M. Rowe Company 1962**
Copyright 1954 By The H. M. Rowe Company

All Rights Reserved
List No. 72
ISBN 0-88294-322-7

Printed in
U. S. A.

CONTENTS

GETTING TO KNOW YOUR TYPEWRITER

How well do you know your typewriter? Take time now to learn where these devices are and how they are used.

PARTS TO HOLD OR RELEASE THE PAPER

Cylinder (also called **platen**)—the roller around which the paper turns.

Paper Rest or Table—the slanted metal plate that supports the paper.

Paper Bail—the long bar above the cylinder with paper holders to keep the paper firm.

Card Holders—the metal or transparent fingers in front of the cylinder used to give added grip.

Paper Release—the lever at the end of the cyl-inder used to relieve pressure on the paper.

PARTS TO MARK PAPER POSITION

Line or Writing Scale—the scale at the front of the machine that shows the spaces in the line.

Paper Guide—the movable metal strip on the paper rest that guides the left edge of the paper.

Paper Guide Scale—the scale on the paper rest that marks the edge of the paper.

Paper Bail Scale—the scale shown on the paper bail to help check writing position.

PARTS TO MOVE THE PAPER UP OR DOWN

Cylinder Knobs—the two large knobs at the ends of the cylinder. Use either knob.

Carriage Return Lever—the long lever extending forward from the left end of the carriage to re-turn the carriage and space to the next line.

Carriage Return Bar or Key—the bar or key on an electric typewriter to return the carriage and space to the next line. It may be located on either side—or on both sides—of the keyboard.

Line Space Regulator—the small knob at the left end of the cylinder to set the vertical spacing.

Variable Line Spacer—the button on the left cyl-inder knob that is used to reset the line.

Ratchet Release—the lever at the left end of the cylinder that permits typing above or below the regular line of writing.

PARTS TO MOVE THE CARRIAGE FROM SIDE TO SIDE

Space Bar—the long bar below the bottom row of keys. Each time you strike this bar, the car-riage moves one space. If you use one additional pressure, some electric typewriters will continue to space until you release the bar. Other electrics have a separate key for repeat forward spacing.

Carriage Release Lever—the lever near each cylinder knob which releases the carriage to per-mit you to move the carriage quickly in either direction.

Backspace Key—the key on the upper left or right of the keyboard. Press to move the carriage back one space. An electric typewriter will con-tinue to backspace until the key is released.

Tabulator Bar or Key—a bar or key that usually is specially marked. When this bar or key is de-pressed, the carriage jumps automatically to the next tabulator setting.

Margin Release—the marked key on the right or left side of the keyboard that permits writing beyond the margin without moving the stop.

PARTS FOR SPECIAL PURPOSES

Ribbon Indicator and Stencil Lever—the lever on the front of the machine with red, blue, and white settings. It is used to raise, lower, or disengage the ribbon.

Touch Tuning or Touch Control—a lever that is usually located on the front part of the machine. It regulates the touch for light, medium, or firm stroking.

Tabulator Set—the marked key on the upper right of the keyboard used to set tabulator stops.

Tabulator Clear—the marked key on the upper left of the keyboard used to clear tabulator stop settings.

Automatic Margin Stop Set—a key or lever that sets the margin stops.

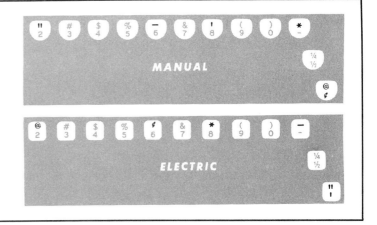
Getting Off to a Good Start

The first part of this text consists of twenty lessons designed to develop your typewriting skill. Following those lessons are twenty Practice Units which train you to apply that skill to your personal and business typing.

On this page and on the next two pages are the ten basic points you need to learn to get off to a good start. They form the beginning of your course. Study them carefully.

1. WATCH YOUR POSTURE. Sit directly in front of your typewriter, so that the letter H is even with the center of your body. You may lean forward slightly if you like, but your general posture should be erect. Let your arms hang naturally from your shoulders.

Keep both feet flat on the floor, with the heel of one foot opposite the toes of the other.

2. HOW TO INSERT PAPER. Pick up the paper with your left hand. Grip the sheet about midway from top to bottom between your thumb and four fingers; then drop it between the paper table and the cylinder of your typewriter.

Grasp the right cylinder knob firmly with the thumb and the first two fingers of your right hand; then give the knob a quick twist or twirl.

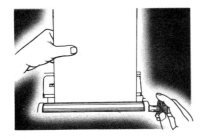

In case the paper needs to be adjusted, depress the paper release lever, straighten the paper by hand, and flip the lever back into position.

3. VERTICAL SPACING. Near the left cylinder knob of your typewriter you will find a small lever with settings marked *1*, *2*, and *3*. Set that lever at *1* for single spacing, at *2* for double spacing, and at *3* for triple spacing.

The carriage return lever (or the carriage return bar or key of an electric typewriter) will turn up the paper one line at a time when the setting is at *1*, two lines at a time when the setting is at *2*, and three lines at a time when the setting is at *3*.

There are six typewriter lines to a vertical inch.

4. PICA AND ELITE TYPE. Does your typewriter have pica type or elite type?

Pica type, which is the larger of the two sizes, provides for ten characters or spaces to the horizontal inch (across the sheet). Elite type provides for twelve characters to the inch.

(Spacing to the horizontal inch is technically called *pitch*. Standard pica is a 10-pitch type.)

5

SPACING CORRECTLY WITH PUNCTUATION MARKS

Period, Question Mark, and Exclamation Point—Space twice after the punctuation mark at the end of a sentence.

```
Is the offer made in good faith?  Of course, it is!  Let us
know whether you are interested.  Can you decide this week?
```

Space once after a period used with an abbreviation unless the abbreviation consists entirely of single lower-case letters.

```
Mr. W. B. Norse and Dr. Barr came at 9:15 a.m. today.
```

Comma—Space once after a comma except when it is used within a number. Do not space after the comma that is part of a number.

```
The shipment made on Monday, June 9, consisted of 7 cases,
90 crates, and 1,216 cartons.
```

Semicolon—Space once after the semicolon.

```
Take time to do good work; neatness always pays.
```

Colon—Space twice after the colon except when it separates hours and minutes. Do not space at all after the colon separating hours and minutes.

```
Take one of these trains:  the 7:32, the 7:50, or the 8:05.
```

Dash—Do not space before, after, or between the hyphens in the formal dash.

```
The officers--Mr. Poe, Mr. Hughes, and Miss Jay--are here.
```

Space once before and once after the hyphen used as an informal dash.

```
The entire amount - not just part of it - is due now.
```

Apostrophe—Do not space before or after an apostrophe that is used within a word.

```
I can't read this person's handwriting.
```

Quotation Marks—Do not space between quotation marks (or single quotation marks) and the material they enclose.

```
"I don't know," she confessed, "why the words 'without
recourse' were included."
```

Parentheses—Space once before the left parenthesis mark and space once after the right parenthesis mark. Do not space between the parentheses and the material they enclose.

```
The only activity shown on the program for the first day
of the convention (Thursday) is a banquet.
```

5. HOW TO SET MARGIN STOPS. Different makes and models of typewriters are equipped with different devices for setting margin stops. In all cases, however, you will proceed in basically the same way when you are using a non-electric typewriter: (1) release or "clear" the margin that is now set; (2) move the carriage to the point on the scale where you want the margin to be; then (3) set the margin at that point.

With some electric typewriters you merely (1) move the carriage to the margin stop and then (2) depress simultaneously the electric margin key and either the repeat forward spacer (to move the stop forward) or the repeat backspacer (to move the stop backward).

Throughout the first eleven lessons you will set only the left margin. The following table shows the correct points at which to set that margin.

First check the paper guide. It should be set to feed the paper into your machine so that the left edge of the sheet will be at zero on the line scale. On most typewriters a zero setting on the paper guide scale lines up with zero on the line scale.

Line Length	Pica Left Margin	Elite Left Margin
40 spaces	23	31
50 spaces	18	26
60 spaces	13	21
70 spaces	8	16

Move the right margin setting all the way to the end until you are told later how to use it.

Note: These settings are for typewriters that have 0 at one *end* of the scale. If you have a Remington with *0* at the *center* of the scale, set the paper guide at the arrow and set the left margin at one-half the number of spaces in the line—at 20 for a 40-space line; at 25 for a 50-space line; and so on.

6. THE HOME KEYS. Look at the keys on the second row from the bottom of the keyboard. The four keys at the far left—A S D and F—are the home keys for the four fingers of your left hand. The keys for J K L and ; are the home keys for your right hand.

In typing by touch, hold your fingers in a curved position over these eight keys.

You will learn to strike each of the other keys on your typewriter by learning how to make the reach from a designated home key. Your finger will start from and return to its home position. One of the first things you need to do, therefore, is to *memorize the home key for each finger.*

	Left Hand		Right Hand
	A—little finger		J—first finger
	S—third finger		K—second finger
	D—second finger		L—third finger
	F—first finger		;—little finger

7. HOW TO HOLD YOUR HANDS. Hold your hands parallel to the slope of the keyboard; then curl your fingers so that they *just about* touch their home keys. Let your wrists drop slightly. If your chair and desk are properly adjusted, the downward slope of your forearms will be at a less pronounced angle than the slope of your hands.

Never let your hands rest on the frame of your typewriter while you are typing.

8. HOW TO STRIKE THE KEYS. Strike each key with the same lightning-like downward and upward movement that a bird uses to peck food from the ground.

Your finger—not your hand—makes the stroke. If you are striking a key in the row above the home row, your finger merely straightens slightly to make the stroke. To strike a key below the home row, your finger draws back slightly. Keep your hands, as far as possible, in a fixed position.

When you are typing on an electric machine, keep your fingers slightly curved, with the palms of your hands parallel to the slope of the keyboard. Just tap the keys.

9. EYES ON COPY! Place your book—or any other copy from which you are typing—at the *right* of your machine if you are using a non-electric typewriter. You may place the copy on either side of an electric machine. Keep your eyes fixed on that copy.

If—during your first lessons—you must refer to the keyboard or to a keyboard chart, do so only when your finger is not striking a key. *Never look at the typewriter keyboard while you are typing.*

APPENDIX

TAKING CARE OF YOUR TYPEWRITER

√ Dust your typewriter daily. Use a soft cloth for surface dust and a long-handled brush for the hard-to-get-at places.

√ Keep the type clean. Use any standard type-cleaning fluid and a stiff brush. Be sure to brush toward you.

√ Clean the cylinder and the paper feed rolls once a week. Use a cloth slightly moistened with type-cleaning fluid or with denatured alcohol.

√ Let the service man oil your typewriter.

√ Use a backing sheet. It will reduce wear on the cylinder and also help to improve the appearance of your typing.

√ Move the carriage to the extreme left or right when you erase to keep eraser shavings from getting into the machine.

√ Keep your typewriter covered when it is not in use.

TYPING SPECIAL CHARACTERS AND SYMBOLS

Name	Example	How Typed
Brackets	$\lfloor \quad \rfloor$	Type underscores in combination with the diagonal.
Caret	$\diagup$	Type an underscore and a diagonal.
Cedilla	ç	Type the comma over the small c.
Chemical Quantity	H_2O	Type the letters first; then turn the cylinder forward slightly to add the number or numbers.
Dash	--	Type two hyphens.
Degree	65°	Turn the cylinder back slightly and type the small o.
Division Sign	÷	Type the colon over the hyphen.
Equals Sign	=	Type the hyphen, roll the cylinder forward slightly, backspace, and strike another hyphen.
Exclamation Point	!	Hold down the space bar and the shift key with your left hand; then type the apostrophe and the period with your right hand.
Exponent	x^2	Turn the cylinder back slightly to type the numeral.
Paragraph Mark	¶	Type parentheses in combination with two underscores.
Plus Sign	+	Type the diagonal over the hyphen.

10. HOW TO RETURN THE CARRIAGE. The carriage return lever on the left side of the carriage is used (1) to turn up to the next line for typing and (2) to return the carriage to the starting point of the line.

If your machine has a downsweep lever, hold your left hand in a vertical position with your fingers extended and strike the lever with the inside of your fingers.

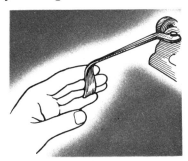

If the lever on your machine is of the upsweep style, hold your left hand palm down—fingers close together—and strike the lever with your first finger.

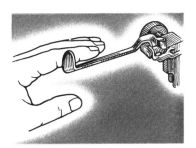

Follow these three steps:

Step 1. Raise your left hand from its home position into position to strike the lever.

Step 2. Strike the lever with a quick, short stroke—just hard enough to space to the next line of writing before actually moving the carriage. Keep your fingers pressed against the lever.

Step 3. Now, with a single, sweeping motion of your hand—still with the palm down—throw the carriage to the starting point and slide your fingers off the lever and back to their home position.

If you are using an electric typewriter, you may keep your fingers on the keyboard when you return the carriage. Just "fan" your fingers to reach the carriage return bar or key. Depress it lightly and quickly. It is not necessary to hold down the bar or key until the carriage reaches the beginning of the next line of writing.

TYPING ON AN ELECTRIC

The most significant difference between an electric and a non-electric machine is difference in touch. Typing on an electric simply requires far less effort. The keys are more sensitive than the keys on a non-electric; they are depressed a shorter distance, and they respond to a much lighter touch.

Until you get used to an electric, concentrate on resting your fingers very lightly on the home keys and on using just enough effort to activate a type bar.

Remember that—on an electric typewriter—the machine itself controls the force of the type-bar strokes. Impressions on the paper are uniform in appearance and density—no matter how hard you strike the keys.

These same observations apply to electric machines with a moving "ball" or typing element instead of type bars. The *RETURN* key returns the typing element instead of the carriage, but the keyboard operation is the same.

PROBLEM 2. The illustration on this page shows a special kind of data sheet. In this case the applicant goes into detail about her business experience.

The facts that will be most interesting to the prospective employer are conveniently arranged to give a quick picture of the applicant's qualifications.

The letter given below is the accompanying letter of application.

Type the letter on an 8½ by 11 sheet of plain paper. Use a 5-inch line.

Start the applicant's home address on the 12th line from the top of the sheet. Leave four blank line spaces below the date.

2048 West 29th Street   Newark, New Jersey   07115

(Today's date)

Box KS-509   Newark Morning Star   Newark, New Jersey   07109

Gentlemen: Please consider this letter as my application for the position that you advertised this morning. ¶ You will notice from the enclosed summary of my business experience that my work for the last eight years has been in the motor freight industry. That experience, I feel confident, has prepared me to take over the duties outlined in your ad. ¶ When I accepted my present position, my residence was in Brooklyn. Because my family has now moved to Newark, I am eager to find work that will reduce the time I spend going to and from work. ¶ I am 27 years old and have fine health. I can supply excellent references from people who know me well and who have had a chance to judge my work. ¶ May I arrange for an interview? You may leave a message for me by calling my home—215-0039. Sincerely yours,   Hazel R. Jeffries   Enclosure

Now type the data sheet from the copy that follows.

Use an 8½ by 11 sheet of paper. Do your typing to a 5-inch line.

Follow the illustration as a model for your work.

Hazel R. Jeffries
2048 West 29th Street
Newark, New Jersey   07115
Telephone—215-0039

SUMMARY OF BUSINESS EXPERIENCE
<u>Employer</u>   King Motor Freight Company, Brooklyn, New York   <u>Service</u> 2½ years (I am employed here now.)   <u>My Work</u> I prepare bills and take care of routine correspondence about bills, credits, and adjustments. During my first six months here, I posted remittances and credits to customers' accounts. <u>Skills</u> My typing speed on straight copy is about 65 words a minute. I operate a Cogswell billing machine and a Davidson calculator. <u>Employer</u> MacVeigh Express Lines, Long Island City, New York   <u>Service</u> 5½ years   <u>My Work</u> When I left here to accept a position at better pay with King, I was tracing shipments and was serving as receptionist and switchboard operator. Before then I did most types of general office work, including filing, posting, and typing from dictation. <u>Skills</u> My shorthand speed is about 110 words a minute.

Building Typing Skill

margin - 25 - 75
50 letter space
Short letters

Use paper of standard 8½-inch width for all your practice work. The material in Lesson 1 will fit on a half sheet—8½ inches wide by 5½ inches deep. For all other lessons, however, be sure to start with a full 8½″ by 11″ sheet.

Always leave a top margin of one inch—six blank lines. To do so, you will space down seven lines from the top edge of the sheet and start typing on the seventh line.

LESSON 1
A S D K L .

Line length for this lesson—50 spaces. Set the left margin stop. Set the line space lever at 1 for single spacing. Type each line in this lesson twice with single spacing. Double-space after each two-line group.

TRAINING YOUR FINGERS. The period is the only key in this lesson that is not on the home row. To type the period, draw the L finger down and slightly to the right. Keep the first finger of your right hand over the J key. You may lift the other fingers slightly.

To make a space, strike the space bar a quick, glancing blow with your *right thumb*. Keep your fingers in home position as you do so.

After you have located the keys, *look away* from the keyboard and "shadow-type" asd *space* kl. *space* (without actually depressing the keys). Continue this practice until the location of each key is firmly fixed in your mind.

KEY LOCATION PRACTICE. Use sharp, staccato strokes. Think each letter as you type it. As far as possible, *move your fingers only*.

asd kl. asd kl. asd kl. aksl dka. asd kl. asd kl.
ask asks add alas all sad lad salad lads lass ad.

Here is how your finished work should look.

```
asd kl. asd kl. asd kl. aksl dka. asd kl. asd kl.
asd kl. asd kl. asd kl. aksl dka. asd kl. asd kl.

ask asks add alas all sad lad salad lads lass ad.
ask asks add alas all sad lad salad lads lass ad.
```

8

```
                    Foster W. Stevens, Jr.
                    56 East Cypress Drive
                    Gulfport, Mississippi  39501
```

PERSONAL DATA

```
Age:  20
Marital Status:  Single
Height:  5'10"
Weight:  152
Health:  Excellent
```

EDUCATION

Graduated from Gulfport Joint High School--General Course.

> My best subjects were Mathematics and English. I was manager of the baseball team during my senior year and president for two years of the Dramatic Club.

Completed two evening courses at Jefferson Junior College.

> I studied Office Management and Effective Speech.

Now attending Oliver Business College three nights a week.

> I am studying Accounting and Mathematics of Business.

EXPERIENCE

Now employed by Triple-A Finance Company in Gulfport.

> My work consists of receiving and crediting the payments of customers. I have held this position for 17 months.

Formerly employed by Logan Advertising Agency in Gulfport.

> When I finished high school, I took temporary work with this agency as an interviewer. I made consumer surveys on the use of a number of household products.

REFERENCES (All by permission)

Dr. Keith Hugh Collins, Jefferson Junior College, Gulfport,
    Mississippi 39503
Mr. Howard N. Gilligan, President, Logan Advertising Agency,
    Gulfport, Mississippi 39501
Mr. Lynn C. LaFarge, 211 Law and Commerce Building, Carr and
    Davis Streets, New Orleans, Louisiana 70114

TYPING CAPITALS. To type a capital, depress the shift key with the little finger of one hand *while* you strike the letter key with the correct finger of the other hand.

To type a capital *A*, for example, (1) depress and hold down the right-hand shift key with the little finger of your right hand; (2) strike the *A* with the little finger of your left hand; then (3) immediately release the shift key.

To reach either shift key easily, keep only your first finger in position as an anchor. Raise the second and third fingers slightly and let them spread fanwise.

SKILL BUILDING. These lines include capital letters. When you release the shift key, bring your little finger back to home position.

```
A. D. Ala. Alaska La. Dallas Dad Ada Salk S. Dak.
D. A. La Las Ladd SS. Sask. Kaska Kalkaska AAA D.
```

SENTENCE WRITING. Always space twice after the period at the end of a sentence. Do not look at the keys while you are typing these sentences!

```
Ask all.  Ask a lass.  Ask a sad lad.  Ladd asks.
Dad asks.  Dad asks a sad lad.  Sal adds a salad.
Lads add.  Al adds.  Dallas asks all.  Ask a lad.
```

Here is how your complete lesson should look.

```
ask kl. asd kl. asd kl. aksl dka. asd kl. asd kl.
asd kl. asd kl. asd kl. aksl dka. asd kl. asd kl.

ask asks add alas all sad lad salad lads lass ad.
ask asks add alas all sad lad salad lads lass ad.

A. D. Ala. Alaska La. Dallas Dad Ada Salk S. Dak.
A. D. Ala. Alaska La. Dallas Dad Ada Salk S. Dak.

D. A. La Las Ladd SS. Sask. Kaska Kalkaska AAA D.
D. A. La Las Ladd SS. Sask. Kaska Kalkaska AAA D.

Ask all.  Ask a lass.  Ask a sad lad.  Ladd asks.
Ask all.  Ask a lass.  Ask a sad lad.  Ladd asks.

Dad asks.  Dad asks a sad lad.  Sal adds a salad.
Dad asks.  Dad asks a sad lad.  Sal adds a salad.

Lads add.  Al adds.  Dallas asks all.  Ask a lad.
Lads add.  Al adds.  Dallas asks all.  Ask a lad.
```

Get into the habit of using the paper release lever when you remove the paper from your machine.

WARM-UP   Mend the big rug for us if it is torn and then lay it down.

ALPHABET   Ask him why few experts recognized valuable antique jewels.

CONTROL   Route 649 is 125 or 130 miles from this town of 780 people.

When you type a letter of application, keep your letter short enough to fit comfortably on one page. If you want to give detailed information about yourself, arrange such data on a separate sheet to accompany your letter.

Use the semiblock style with mixed punctuation for your letter. Group the facts on your data sheet to make them easy to read and to give the sheet a pleasing appearance.

Try to put yourself in the position of your prospective employer. Present those facts that will help him to decide whether you have the background and the personality to fit you for the work that he needs to have done.

Until you have an interview, the only clue that your prospective employer has of your neatness and accuracy as a worker is your letter of application. Take pains to see that he gets a pleasing first impression.

Whether or not you give references in your letter of application depends upon the special circumstances under which you are making the application. Often the references may be supplied later—at the time of your interview. In any case, be sure you have permission from the persons whose names you are using before you give their names as references.

PROBLEM 1. Type the following application letter on an 8½ by 11 sheet of plain paper. When you have finished the letter, turn to the next page and make a copy of the accompanying data sheet.

Use a 5-inch line for the letter. Start the applicant's home address on the 11th line from the top edge of the sheet. Leave four blank line spaces below the date. (In case you need to review the typing of personal-business letters, turn

back to Practice Unit 6, page 60, and read over the model letter, page 61.)

Type the data sheet to a line length of 6 inches. Leave a 1-inch top margin. Triple-space before each of the four main divisions.

56 East Cypress Drive   **Gulfport, Mississippi 39501** *(Today's date)*

Mr. David Lorden, Personnel Director   Gulf Coast Tea and Spice Company   Dock Street at Third Avenue   New Orleans, Louisiana 70116 Dear Mr. Lorden: This morning Mr. Carter Loomis, your District Sales Manager, telephoned me to tell me that there will soon be an opening on your sales force in the Gulfport area.   Please consider me an applicant for that position.   ¶ Mr. Loomis has been a family friend for years.   He will, I know, recommend me to you.   Meantime, I am rushing this letter to you by special delivery, so that you will have an opportunity to consider me before you decide on a man for this territory.   ¶ The enclosed sheet summarizes my background.   I am also attaching a recent photograph.   ¶ Although I have every reason to believe that my present employer is well pleased with me, I am unable to see any opportunity here for advancement.   I am eager to find work that offers me a future and that will bring me into contact with customers.   I enjoy working with people.   ¶ Will it be convenient for me to telephone you and to talk over the position with you?   After you have talked with me, I hope that I may come to New Orleans for an interview.   Sincerely yours,   Foster W. Stevens, Jr. Enclosures 2

Line length for this lesson—50 spaces. Set the left margin stop. Type each line on this page twice with single spacing. Double-space after each two-line group.

WARM-UP REVIEW. These lines include all the strokes you learned in Lesson 1. Space twice after a period at the end of a sentence.

```
Ask a lad.  Dad asks all.  Dad asks all sad lads.
Dad asks a sad lass.  Ask a lass.  Ladd adds all.
```

TRAINING YOUR FINGERS. Four of the keys in this lesson are on the third row. To strike a key on the third row, straighten your finger slightly, but *do not move your hand or arm forward.* Keep at least one finger in home position. You may lift the other fingers slightly to help you make the reach comfortably.

Locate the keys. Then look away from the keyboard and "shadow-type" erf *space* jip *space* for a few moments.

Left Hand
E—Use D finger
R—Use F finger

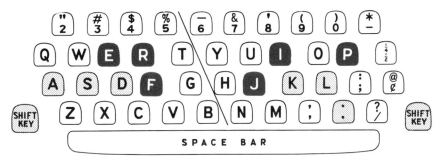

Right Hand
I—Use K finger
P—Use ; finger

KEY LOCATION PRACTICE. Think each letter as you strike the key; then bring your finger back to home position. *Do not look at the keyboard.*

```
erf jip erf jip erf jip ejri fjep erf jip erf jip
rid ride rip ripe rifle if life jar par park pies
are pare jerk jeer peer keep field fir fire spire
```

SKILL BUILDING. These sentences contain all the letters you have now learned. Are you sitting far enough back from your machine?

```
Keep a jar.  Ride a spare sled if all else fails.
I said a park is like a field.  Keep a ripe pear.
Add a spire.  I like all parks.  Rides are risks.
A field is afire.  Fire a rifle if a lass is ill.
Jasper did fire a rifle.  A lass led a sled ride.
Park riders jeer pale lads.  A jade jar is liked.
Ed led raids.  Sell fields.  Keep all apple pies.
```

WALTER MARTINDALE HONORED
BY CITY'S BUSINESS LEADERS

At last week's anniversary dinner of the Business and Industry Club, Walter Martindale was named Athlete of the Year and presented with the Club's coveted annual plaque for outstanding sportsmanship.

George V. Steele, President of the Club, made the presentation. He cited Martindale as a "champion through and through--a man whose modesty is every bit as great as his spectacular record in sports."

In accepting the award, the star praised his team mates and Coach Larry Griffin, who was a special guest at the banquet. "Nobody wins alone," Martindale said. "The real thrill of playing is the thrill of being part of a great team."

Martindale is the third man to be selected for the B & I Club award. Previous winners are Steve Wood and Frank Long.

PICNIC AND OUTING SCHEDULED
FOR JUNE AT RIVERSIDE BEACH

Saturday, June 24, is the date selected for this year's picnic and outing, according to an announcement just made by Grover Dean, Chairman of the Program Committee. Arrangements have been made to hold the affair at Riverside Beach. ¶ The program of events will run from noon to dark. Games and contests are slated for the afternoon. Included will be a "Mystery" contest. Dean says that only the Committee knows what it is, and "they're not talking." "If you miss this one," he insists, "you'll miss the biggest laugh of your life." ¶ Also new this year will be an old-fashioned song fest led by the Barber Shop Quartette in Gay Nineties attire. ¶ Letters will be mailed to members to give full plans. Just be sure to mark the date!

PROBLEM 2. Type the two column-width articles in this Practice Unit with justified right margins side by side on a full-size sheet of paper.

Note the following illustration.

The article that has been worked out for you goes at the left. The article you typed in Problem 1 goes at the right.

Make each column 3 inches wide (30 pica spaces or 36 elite spaces), and leave 3 spaces between columns. Plan margin and tabulator settings carefully to center your work horizontally on the sheet.

Leave a 2-inch top margin.

Single-space. Double-space after the headings and after each paragraph.

Indent paragraphs 3 spaces.

PROBLEM 1. Type the following article in column width on a full-size sheet of paper.

Use a 3-inch column (30 pica spaces or 36 elite spaces). Center the column horizontally on the sheet. Leave a top margin of 2 inches.

Set a tabulator stop for 3-space paragraph indentions. Single-space, but leave a blank line space after the heading and after each paragraph.

Fill out short lines with asterisks.

When you have finished your typing, make checkmarks at the points where you will put the extra spaces to justify the right margin. Then keep your work for use in Problem 2.

WORD DRILL. You can build speed by typing by letter groups—without thinking of individual letters. Use that technique here.

```
air fair pair aid said laid raids ail fails rails
pail paid repair pad spade spar spare spark paper
led fled sled leak leap lead plea plead sale pale
risk risks rise arise pride drip rips dried fried
ape pear pears pearl spear speak sped spell peril
lake flake fake rake drake like likes alike spike
```

SENTENCE WRITING. These speed-building sentences include many words you just practiced. Try to type by letter groups—not letter by letter.

{Choose one line and practice it}

```
I fled.  Ida likes lake air.  All risks are fair.
Fire a rifle.  Sell a spare pearl.  Repair a rip.
Dad led a fake raid.  Ella said pride is a peril.
Sallie pares ripe apples.  Pearl did rip a paper.
Jeff likes all pies.  Dried paper is a fire risk.
A spike did rip a paper pad.  I like pear salads.
———1———2———3———4———5———6———7———8———9———
```

Finding Your Typing Speed

To simplify the checking of typing speed, five strokes are counted as one word.

Note the numbered scale under the sentences on this page. It counts off the 5-stroke words for you, so that you can find your typing rate quickly. In this lesson, for example, each line contains ten standard words.

A Sentence Writing section is part of each lesson. The sentences in that group are ideal for checking speed because they let you type at your best rate.

To find your speed, select one line from the Sentence Writing section and type it continuously for one minute. Then use the word-count scale to find the number of standard words you typed.

Let us say, for example, that you had typed one of the above lines twice and had reached the 3-word marker on the third typing by the end of one minute. You typed at the rate of 10 plus 10 plus 3, or 23 words a minute.

You may find some lines of a Sentence Writing group slightly faster than others. When time permits, try to better your rate on another line.

Do not expect to type the other sections of the lesson at your Sentence Writing rate. Bear in mind that some of those sections are designed to make you concentrate on accurate stroking. Others are intended to get you used to working with paragraphs that combine fast and slow combinations.

WARM-UP   They may turn to their neighbor for aid with their problem.

ALPHABET   Go quiz an expert driver who can adjust brake drums fairly.

CONTROL   Do 16 problems from page 398 and 25 problems from page 407.

When news bulletins for clubs or organizations, school newspapers, or reports are planned in column form, the appearance is greatly improved by justifying ("evening up") the right margin.

Here are the three steps in typing a column with a justified right margin.

Step 1. Set your machine for the exact width of the column and then type the copy with regular spacing. Fill out short lines with asterisks. The asterisks show the number of extra spaces.

Step 2. Decide where to put the extra spaces and make checkmarks at those points. Try to distribute the spaces as evenly as possible across the line. An extra space is least noticeable when it follows a punctuation mark.

Step 3. Now retype the copy, inserting a space for each checkmark.

A long column heading may be justified. A heading that is considerably shorter than the column should be centered. In the illustration below, the heading has been justified to a column width of 30 spaces. Turn to the top of the next page to see the same heading centered over a column of 36 spaces.

```
WALTER MARTINDALE HONORED*****
BY CITY'S BUSINESS LEADERS****

     At last week's anniversary*
dinner of the Business and In-
dustry Club, Walter Martindale
was named Athlete of the Year*
and presented with the Club's*
coveted annual plaque for out-
standing sportsmanship.

     George V. Steele, President
of the Club, made the presen-*
tation.  He cited Martindale**
as a "champion through and****
through--a man whose modesty**
is every bit as great as his**
spectacular record in sports."

     In accepting the award, the
star praised his team mates***
and Coach Larry Griffin, who**
was a special guest at the****
banquet."  Nobody wins alone,"
Martindale said.  "The real***
thrill of playing is the******
thrill of being part of a*****
great team."

     Martindale is the third man
to be selected for the B & I**
Club award.  Previous winners*
are Steve Wood and Frank Long.
```

Step 1

```
WALTER MARTINDALE HONORED*****
BY CITY'S BUSINESS LEADERS****

     At last week's anniversary*
dinner of the Business and In-
dustry Club, Walter Martindale
was named Athlete of the Year*
and presented with the Club's*
coveted annual plaque for out-
standing sportsmanship.

     George V. Steele, President
of the Club, made the presen-*
tation.  He cited Martindale**
as a "champion through and****
through--a man whose modesty**
is every bit as great as his**
spectacular record in sports."

     In accepting the award, the
star praised his team mates***
and Coach Larry Griffin, who**
was a special guest at the****
banquet.  "Nobody wins alone,"
Martindale said.  "The real***
thrill of playing is the******
thrill of being part of a*****
great team."

     Martindale is the third man
to be selected for the B & I**
Club award.  Previous winners*
are Steve Wood and Frank Long.
```

Step 2

```
WALTER    MARTINDALE    HONORED
BY    CITY'S    BUSINESS    LEADERS

     At last  week's anniversary
dinner of the Business and In-
dustry Club, Walter Martindale
was named  Athlete of the Year
and presented  with the Club's
coveted annual plaque for out-
standing sportsmanship.

     George V. Steele, President
of the Club,  made the presen-
tation.  He cited  Martindale
as a "champion through and
through--a man whose modesty
is  every bit as great as  his
spectacular record in sports."

     In accepting the award, the
star  praised  his  team mates
and  Coach Larry Griffin,  who
was a special  guest at  the
banquet.  "Nobody wins alone,"
Martindale said.    "The real
thrill  of  playing  is  the
thrill  of  being part of  a
great team."

     Martindale is the third man
to be selected for the B  &  I
Club award.    Previous winners
are Steve Wood and Frank Long.
```

Step 3

Line length for this lesson—50 spaces. Set the left margin stop. Set the line space lever at 1. Type each line on this page twice with single spacing. Double-space after each two-line group.

WARM-UP REVIEW. These lines include all strokes you have learned.

Jasper likes red pear pies. Fred likes all pies.
Jeff sells red pails. Fred dislikes pear salads.

TRAINING YOUR FINGERS. Move your fingers back and forth several times between home position and the new keys *without depressing the keys.* Look at the keyboard as you do so to get a mental picture of each reach. For the reaches to *g* and *h*, you should keep only your little finger in position.

Then practice "shadow typing" **wtg** *space* **yho** *space* several times without looking at the keys. If you do need to look at the keyboard, *stop* your "shadow typing" while you look.

Left Hand
W—Use S finger
T —Use F finger
G —Use F finger

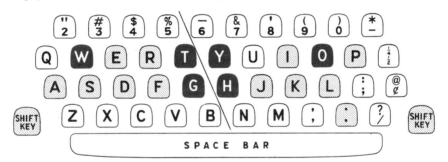

Right Hand
Y —Use J finger
H—Use J finger
O—Use L finger

KEY LOCATION PRACTICE. Bring your finger right back to home position after you strike a key on the third row. Return the carriage snappily, but avoid unnecessary force.

wtg yho wtg yho wtg yho whty ghwo wtg yho wtg yho
go got hot hog how row grow to toy tot owe yellow
yet who why what pay day weight with the they two

SKILL BUILDING. These sentences use the new strokes extensively. They also review all the strokes you learned in Lessons 1 and 2.

The two girls owe for the toy they got a day ago.
A row of yellow roses is what she wishes to grow.
Go with the two lads to help with the yellow jar.
I say it is yet so early for the day to grow hot.
Pay for the hog if the weight is what he did say.
How they got a hot fire is what he asked the tot.
It is he who asked why they did hope to grow hay.

Margins. Leave a top margin of two inches on the first page and a top margin of an inch and one-half on all other pages. Side and bottom margins should be one inch on all pages.

You will be wise to put a light pencil mark about an inch and one-half from the bottom of the sheet before you start. In case you find that a one-inch margin on that particular page will cause a bad break in the text, you can then end the page a line or two sooner than you normally would. Try to avoid a bottom margin that is less than one inch.

Will your manuscript be bound? If so, add one-half inch to the margin along which the binding will be done.

Numbering Pages. Number the pages with Arabic numerals, but omit the number on the first page. Type the page number at least one-half inch from the top edge.

When the manuscript has introductory pages, such as a preface or a table of contents, those pages should be numbered with small Roman numerals (ii, iii, iv, etc.) one-half inch from the bottom.

Quotations. Quotations should be indented five spaces from each margin and typed with single spacing.

> Quotations of several lines should be indented but need not be enclosed with quotation marks. Remember to set a tabulator stop for the indention of paragraphs in the quotation itself.

Side Headings. Headings for subdivisions are often used in manuscripts to help the reader locate certain topics. Different styles are in use. One of the easiest and best styles is the one used in this article. It is called a "run-in" side heading.

WORD DRILL. Some combinations of letters will appear more often than others in your typing. One of the best ways to build your typing speed is to practice those combinations until you can type each one automatically—without thinking of the individual letters.

Each of the following lines consists of familiar words that contain the same letter combination. As you continue your speed-building work in this book, you will get practice on more and more such high-frequency combinations.

```
soot foot root roof door food wood wool tool took
lay slay play delay ray pray way hay say gay stay
ago good goose goat gold golf gorge gospel gossip
three thrifty thrift thrill throw throat throttle
show slow slowly lowly prow prowl growl fowl howl
lot slot pot spot dot dote shot forgot other trot
```

SENTENCE WRITING. These sentences will help you to type at your best rate. They include many of the words you have just practiced.

```
Two girls took a lot of hay to the goat for food.
A thrifty worker took the good wood to that spot.
He forgot hay or other food for their lowly goat.
Show the pair how thrifty it is to grow the food.
Their food slowly got hot while they played golf.
They say she took the pot of gold three days ago.
    1     2     3     4     5     6     7     8     9
```

Check Your Typing Habits!

Good typing habits pay dividends in speed and accuracy. Are you forming these habits?

- Are you striking the keys with firm, snappy strokes?

- Are you keeping your eyes on the copy and off the keyboard while you are typing?

- Do you keep home position with at least one finger when you shift for capitals?

- While you are typing, do you concentrate on what you are doing?

- Are you keeping your hands and arms almost stationary and letting your fingers do the work?

- Have you learned to twirl a sheet of paper into the machine?

- Are you returning the carriage snappily?

- Are you sitting properly?

- Do you have your fingers curled when they are at home position?

Every *No* answer is a danger signal! Work to change it to a positive *Yes*.

TYPING MANUSCRIPTS

The following suggestions will help you to type manuscripts in acceptable form. Study them carefully.

Paper. Use standard 8½" by 11" white paper of good quality. Select paper on which you can erase. Type on one side only.

Carbon Copies. Make at least one carbon copy. Determine the exact number of copies that will be needed before you start.

Spacing. Use double spacing for the main text of the manuscript. Leave an extra interline below the heading. Use single spacing for footnotes and for indented quotations.

Footnotes. A footnote should be indicated in the text of the manuscript by means of a superior figure. A matching superior figure precedes the footnote at the bottom of the page. To type the superior figures, use the ratchet release.

Single-space each footnote. Double-space between footnotes. Using the underscore, type a solid line to separate the last line of the text from the footnote or footnotes. To center that solid line, space once before typing it and space twice afterwards.

The arrangement of the material in a footnote that refers to a book[1] differs from the arrangement of the material in a footnote that refers to a magazine article.[2] Note examples on this page.

---

[1]David R. Man, Manuscripts, Bard Press, Detroit, 1962, p. 9.

[2]Gladys D. LeSeur, "Typists at Work," Business Forum Monthly, April, 1962, pp. 29-32.

LESSON 4
Q C V U N M

Line length for this lesson—50 spaces. Set the left margin stop. Set the line space lever at 1 until you are told to move it. Type each line on this page twice with single spacing. Double-space after each two-line group.

WARM-UP REVIEW. These lines include all the strokes you have learned so far.

```
Gladys asked her father to ship the jewel to her.
Alfred likes rolls filled with fresh grape jelly.
```

TRAINING YOUR FINGERS. Check the location of each new key. While you look at the keyboard, practice making each reach without depressing the key. To strike *q* with the little finger of your left hand, lift your second and third fingers slightly. Keep the first finger in home position.

After you "get the feel" of the new reaches, *look away from the keyboard* and "shadow-type" qcv *space* unm *space*. Continue that "shadow typing" for several moments.

Left Hand
Q—Use A finger
C—Use D finger
V—Use F finger

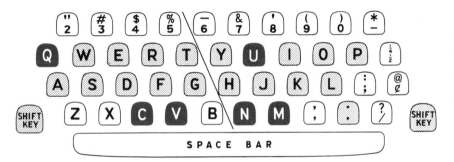

Right Hand
U—Use J finger
N—Use J finger
M—Use J finger

KEY LOCATION PRACTICE. Think each letter as you strike the key! Concentrate on the key location and on the finger you are using.

```
qcv unm qcv unm qcv unm cuvn qucm qcv unm qcv unm
an man van can cane main vain came name come cove
menu quay qualm queen quick run fun sun tune dune
```

SKILL BUILDING. These sentences give you applied practice with the new strokes. They also review all strokes from the earlier lessons.

```
It is fun to hear the vain man play a quick tune.
Name that main cove for the man who came for fun.
Run quickly down the menu and pick a main course.
One man ran in the sun from our quay to the cove.
Jan can come to a gay fair to name the new queen.
The vain man may name an old van for his one son.
Make that man use a cane if he comes up the dune.
```

WARM-UP Title to the island is held by an heir of the rich visitor.

ALPHABET Jay never paid the boys for glazing exquisite ceramic work.

CONTROL The 65 boys and 128 girls have now sold 739 or 740 tickets.

The illustrations on this page show how to arrange the pages of a theme or of a manuscript.

Notice that a line length of 6½ inches is recommended. That length provides adequate side margins and yet permits good use of the available space on the page.

In case you will bind your theme or manuscript, you will, of course, adjust the margins. If the binding is to be done along the left edge, increase the left margin to 1½ inches. If you will bind at the top, increase the top margin by one-half inch.

The position of the page number depends in part upon personal preference and in part upon the way the manuscript will be bound. In case you will bind the manuscript at the side, you may —if you like—move the page number to the upper right-hand corner of the page, where it will be even with the right margin. For a manuscript bound at the top, you may either lower the page number a half-inch or you may move it to the bottom margin.

The page number in the illustration below was centered and typed one-half inch from the top edge of the sheet.

There is just one "rule" that you should always follow in typing page numbers: *Leave at least two interlines between the page number and the nearest line of the text.*

The next two pages in this book are models of the first and second pages of a manuscript that will not be bound. Those pages also contain instructions for arranging your work in good form. Study them before you do any typing.

PROBLEM 1. Type the following two pages— TYPING MANUSCRIPTS. Use a 5-space paragraph indention.

These pages were originally typed in pica type on 8½ by 11 sheets and then reduced slightly. In case you are using a pica machine, therefore, you will copy them line for line.

In case you have an elite machine, remember that you will be typing to a 78-space line and that you will get more material on your first page than there is on the first model page. Watch your bottom margin!

Remember, too, to leave enough space to type the footnotes.

TYPING MANUSCRIPTS

The following suggestions will help you to type manuscripts in acceptable form. Study them carefully.

Paper. Use standard 8½" by 11" white paper of good quality. Select paper on which you can erase. Type on one side only.

Carbon Copies. Make at least one carbon copy. Determine the exact number of copies that will be needed before you start.

Spacing. Use double spacing for the main text of the manuscript. Leave an extra interline below the heading. Use single spacing for footnotes and for indented quotations.

Footnotes. A footnote should be indicated in the text of the manuscript by means of a superior figure. A matching superior figure precedes the footnote at the bottom of the page. To type the superior figures, use the ratchet release.

Single-space each footnote. Double-space between footnotes. Using the underscore, type a solid line to separate the last line of the text from the footnote or footnotes. To center that solid line, space once before typing it and space twice afterwards.

The arrangement of the material in a footnote that refers to a book[1] differs from the arrangement of the material in a footnote that refers to a magazine article.[2] Note examples on this page.

[1]David R. Man, *Manuscripts*, Bard Press, Detroit, 1962, p. 9.
[2]Gladys D. LeSeur, "Typists at Work," *Business Forum Monthly*, April, 1962, pp. 29-32.

Top Margin

2 inches on first page; 1½ inches on other pages.

Side Margins

1-inch left and right margins on all pages. Use 65-space pica line or 78-space elite line.

Bottom Margin

1 inch on all pages.

2

Margins. Leave a top margin of two inches on the first page and a top margin of an inch and one-half on all other pages. Side and bottom margins should be one inch on all pages.

You will be wise to put a light pencil mark about an inch and one-half from the bottom of the sheet before you start. In case you find that a one-inch margin on that particular page will cause a bad break in the text, you can then end the page a line or two sooner than you normally would. Try to avoid a bottom margin that is less than one inch.

Will your manuscript be bound? If so, add one-half inch to the margin along which the binding will be done.

Numbering Pages. Number the pages with Arabic numerals, but omit the number on the first page. Type the page number at least one-half inch from the top edge.

When the manuscript has introductory pages, such as a preface or a table of contents, those pages should be numbered with small Roman numerals (ii, iii, iv, etc.) one-half inch from the bottom.

Quotations. Quotations should be indented five spaces from each margin and typed with single spacing.

Quotations of several lines should be indented but need not be enclosed with quotation marks. Remember to set a tabulator stop for the indention of paragraphs in the quotation itself.

Side Headings. Headings for subdivisions are often used in manuscripts to help the reader locate certain topics. Different styles are in use. One of the easiest and best styles is the one used in this article. It is called a "run-in" side heading.

Speed Building

Type twice—with single spacing—each line of Word Drill, Sentence Writing, and Paragraph Preview. Double-space after each two-line group.

WORD DRILL. Practice on these letter combinations will help you pick up speed. Each combination includes at least one of the new strokes.

```
dove move love glove clove rove drove prove shove
men omen women mend lament payment mental mention
cut cute cutlet cur cure curt curl curio cue cult
haul maul fault vault rule truly dull full sullen
quake quaint quail quack quality quantity qualify
done gone tone stone atone lone alone drone shone
```

SENTENCE WRITING. Many of the words you have just practiced are included in these speed-building sentences.

```
Move that quaint curio to the vault when you can.
Men and women who truly qualify ask full payment.
That curt man and the sullen woman have now gone.
Haul the lone stone here to prove that it is cut.
Mention of an omen makes many of the women quake.
Mend a glove for that woman who drove here alone.
```
——— 1 ——— 2 ——— 3 ——— 4 ——— 5 ——— 6 ——— 7 ——— 8 ——— 9 ———

PARAGRAPH PREVIEW. Concentrate as you type these words. Strive for accuracy. This practice will increase your speed on the paragraph that ends the lesson.

Practice

```
downward upward pecking striking using strike try
food good snappy will fowls movement proper quick
```

PARAGRAPH TYPING. *Set the line space lever at 2.* Type this paragraph once—line for line—with double spacing. It contains all the strokes you have learned.

	Words
You should strike each key with a firm and snappy	10
stroke if it is your just desire to do good work.	20
You will find it worth your while if you will try	30
to learn the proper way of striking the keys from	40
the start. Try using the same quick downward and	50
upward movement that fowls use when pecking food.	60

——— 1 ——— 2 ——— 3 ——— 4 ——— 5 ——— 6 ——— 7 ——— 8 ——— 9 ———

PROBLEM 3. Prepare the announcement shown below for duplication on a 5½ by 8½ half sheet.

Leave a 1-inch top margin. Set margin stops for a line of 3½ inches.

Center the heading and the two lines at the bottom of the sheet. Space out and underscore the words in the first line of the heading.

Triple-space after the heading and before and after the final paragraph. Double-space after the other paragraphs.

Set a tabulator stop for the indented paragraphs in the body of the announcement. Be sure that the stop provides for two blank spaces after the *longest* side heading.

F a m i l y   O u t i n g

of the

LARCHMONT COMMUNITY ASSOCIATION

When?   Saturday, August 22, from
         11 a.m. until ....

Where?   Logan's Picnic Park, Willow
         Road, 2½ miles north of Memo-
         rial Highway. Follow signs.

What?   Fun galore for everybody!
         Swimming...soft ball...boat
         rides...dancing...games and
         swings for the kiddies.

Eats?   Delicious picnic fare. You
         can count on extra helpings
         if you want them.

Cost?   Here's the best news of all.
         Adult tickets are only $2--
         and that amount pays every-
         thing. Youngsters come free.

Call Milton Taft right away for your
tickets--322-9154. No tickets will
be sold at the park.

Remember the date!

Come and have fun!

LESSON 5

Timed Typing

Line length for this lesson—50 spaces. Set the left margin stop. Set the line space lever at 1. The paragraphs on this page give you an opportunity to time yourself on continuous typing for a period of several minutes. Omit the numbers when you type the paragraphs.

PREVIEW PRACTICE. Type each line of words twice. Double-space after each two-line group. The words have been selected from the Continuous Typing material that follows.

```
acquire anything typing thoughts distract focused
upon quick results wondering project glance space
decide despair precious practice up reject wander
see keep error look skill all well rather produce
```

CONTINUOUS TYPING. *Move the line space lever to 2.* Type these paragraphs line for line. Each paragraph contains all the strokes you have learned. Note that the word count is given for the entire article, as well as for individual paragraphs.

Words

1

	Words
You may never do so well as you should if you let	10
your mind wander and your thoughts roam while you	20
are typing. One of the musts for fine results in	30
typing or in any other work that you decide to do	40
is a mind that is focused on the task that is now	50
at hand. Acquire the precious art of making your	60
mind reject anything which may distract you.	69

——1——2——3——4——5——6——7——8——9——

2

		Words
You must learn to keep your eyes on the copy from	10	79
which you are typing and to rely upon the strokes	20	89
to produce the right results for you. One of the	30	99
sure ways to lose time and to have your speed cut	40	109
down is to glance up from time to time to see how	50	119
the work looks on the paper. Very often a stroke	60	129
or space error results from just one quick look.	70	139

——1——2——3——4——5——6——7——8——9——

3

		Words
Most of those who fail some project or who do not	10	149
quite reach the goal they have set are people who	20	159
quit rather early. Keep that fact in mind if you	30	169
start wondering how much time it can take for you	40	179
to acquire the skill that you want or in case you	50	189
now and then have the feeling of despair that may	60	199
come to all of us when we must practice more.	69	208

——1——2——3——4——5——6——7——8——9——

FILL-IN FORM LETTERS. Fill-in form letters are great time-savers for many kinds of routine correspondence. The main part of the letter is duplicated. The date, the inside address, and the salutation, together with other individualized copy, are then typed into the letter.

Compare the "before" and "after" illustrations at the bottom of this page. The illustration at the left shows the duplicated portions of the letter; the one at the right shows the same letter after the individually typed copy has been added.

PROBLEM 1. Prepare the following form letter for duplication on a 5½ by 8½ letterhead. Use the illustration below as a model.

Set margins for a 3½-inch line. Set a tabulator stop for a 5-space paragraph indention.

Start the first paragraph on the 21st line from the top edge of the letterhead.

Note: Your Workbook contains two letterheads marked Form 17-1. Use one of those letterheads for your typing. You may use the other one to run off a copy of the letter from your stencil.

This note is a reminder about your life insurance policy. ¶ The next premium on your policy comes due very soon. Because I know you want to keep your insurance in full force,

I am enclosing a stamped envelope for you to use in mailing your check in good time. ¶ The due date is ¶ Your premium is ¶ Please write your check to the order of Baker & Watts Agency. Sincerely yours, Jerome T. Baker *(Use your own identifying initials.)* **Enclosure**

PROBLEM 2. From the copy given below, fill in the form letter that you have just prepared. Before you start to type, make sure that the material you insert will line up perfectly with the rest of the letter.

Date the letter July 8 (this year). Start at the center two line spaces below the letterhead.

Space back carefully from the first line of the body to get the correct starting line for the inside address. Remember to count the interlines.

Mr. James W. Leggett
2309 Fourth Avenue
Columbus, Ohio   43216

Dear Mr. Leggett:

#274-950.
July 20.
$34.80.

Baker & Watts Agency

· · · · · · · GENERAL INSURANCE AGENTS · · · · · · ·

480 Main Street, Columbus, Ohio   43205

```
            This note is a reminder about
     your life insurance policy

            The next premium on your policy
     comes due very soon.  Because I know
     you want to keep your insurance in
     full force, I am enclosing a stamped
     envelope for you to use in mailing
     your check in good time.

            The due date is

            Your premium is

            Please write your check to the
     order of Baker & Watts Agency.

                    Sincerely yours,


                    Jerome T. Baker

     xx

     Enclosure
```

Baker & Watts Agency

· · · · · · · GENERAL INSURANCE AGENTS · · · · · · ·

480 Main Street, Columbus, Ohio   43205

```
                    July 8, 19--


     Mr. James W. Leggett
     2309 Fourth Avenue
     Columbus, Ohio  43216

     Dear Mr. Leggett:

            This note is a reminder about
     your life insurance policy #274-950.

            The next premium on your policy
     comes due very soon.  Because I know
     you want to keep your insurance in
     full force, I am enclosing a stamped
     envelope for you to use in mailing
     your check in good time.

            The due date is July 20.

            Your premium is $34.80.

            Please write your check to the
     order of Baker & Watts Agency.

                    Sincerely yours,


                    Jerome T. Baker

     xx

     Enclosure
```

WORD DRILL. Practice on these lines will help you to type by letter combinations—rather than by individual letters. Feel your speed improve!

```
depend commend tend lend mend rend send wend vend
defend pretend attend ascend append amend suspend
ending lending mending spending tending defending
make rake take wake awake drake shake snake quake
caking faking making raking taking waking shaking
awaking forsaking mistaking partaking undertaking
```

SENTENCE WRITING. These sentences make wide use of the words you have just practiced. Watch for the high-frequency letter combinations.

```
Take time to defend the lending and the spending.
The raking or shaking may tend to end the caking.
Depend on any man they may send to mend the rake.
Make them pretend to suspend the gay undertaking.
Commend her for making him attend and stay awake.
Pretend to shake the snake to make it come awake.
——1——2——3——4——5——6——7——8——9——
```

PARAGRAPH PREVIEW. Concentrate on your stroking as you type each line the first time; then try to speed up on the second typing of the line.

```
you your small will at attempt amount avoid twirl
learn right rapidly slowly paper patience machine
```

PARAGRAPH TYPING. *Set the line space lever at 2.* Type this paragraph line for line with double spacing. It contains all the words you just practiced.

	Words
You should learn how to twirl the paper into your	10
machine with your fingers and hardly any movement	20
of your arm. Just a small amount of patience and	30
practice will make your skill grow rapidly. Make	40
sure right now that you must avoid any attempt at	50
grinding the paper slowly into your machine.	59

```
——1——2——3——4——5——6——7——8——9——
```

WARM-UP   They dug their own coal and kept half of it for their fuel.

ALPHABET   Clark may quiz the janitor about loading expensive flowers.

CONTROL   By 1960 their company owned 237 or 238 stores in 154 towns.

TYPING MATERIAL FOR REPRODUCTION. Offices, clubs, and other organizations often distribute letters and announcements that are run off in quantity on a duplicating machine. The following suggestions will guide you in typing a stencil for reproducing such material.

1. Always type the material first on a sheet of plain paper. You will then have a placement guide for cutting the stencil.

2. Give your typewriter keys a thorough cleaning with a stiff brush before you start to type on the stencil.

3. Disengage the ribbon by moving the ribbon lever indicator to the "stencil" position.

4. Put the cushion sheet between the stencil sheet and the backing sheet; then insert the assembled pack into your machine. Use the paper release.

5. Make sure that the stencil is perfectly straight. The best way is to line up the first point on the scale that is printed on the stencil with the alignment scale on your typewriter.

6. Strike the keys with a firm, staccato touch. Strike with more than usual force any key that has a particularly large printing surface (such as the $, %, W, M, and E). Use less than usual force in striking the period, the comma, and other keys that have small printing surfaces (like the o, e, c, and l).

7. Be careful to keep your typing within the border marked on the stencil.

8. To make a correction, turn up the stencil a few lines to provide working room and then rub the error with the burnisher. Apply a thin coat of correction fluid to the area. When the fluid is dry, return the stencil to the line of writing and strike the correct keys.

The problems in this Practice Unit are typical examples of duplicated material. Type them in the regular way; then, if stencils are available, cut stencils and run off copies.

USING HALF SHEETS. You have learned to center your typing on full 8½ x 11 sheets and on half sheets that are 8½ inches wide and 5½ inches deep. You need also to become thoroughly familiar with typing on half sheets that are turned the other way.

Study the following diagram.

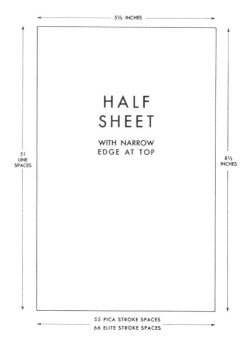

TYPING ON HALF-SIZE LETTERHEADS. Use a 3½-inch line for all letters typed on half-size letterheads that have the narrow edge at the top. You will thus have 1-inch left and right margins. Raise or lower the starting point to get good vertical placement on letters of different lengths.

LESSON 6
Z X B , ;

Line length for this lesson—50 spaces. Set the left margin stop. Set the line space lever at 1 until you are told to move it. Type each line on this page twice with single spacing. Double-space after each two-line group.

WARM-UP REVIEW. These sentences review all the strokes you have learned so far.

```
Jack quickly noticed the fiery volcano eruptions.
Give him ten of the torn maps which they sent us.
```

TRAINING YOUR FINGERS. Locate the new keys. All except the semi-colon are on the bottom row.

When you strike *z*, you may lift the second and third fingers to avoid strain. Keep home position with your first finger.

Strike the comma with the second finger of your right hand. To make that stroke easily, raise your first finger slightly.

While you look at the keyboard, practice making each reach without depressing the key. Then *look away from the keyboard* and "shadow-type" zxb *space* , ; *space* several times.

Left Hand
Z—Use A finger
X—Use S finger
B—Use F finger

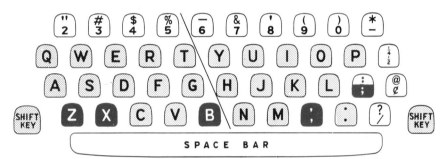

Right Hand
,—Use K finger
;—Use ; finger

KEY LOCATION PRACTICE. As you type these lines, avoid the time-wasting habit of moving all your fingers to the bottom row.

```
zxb ,; zxb ,; zxb ,; b,x ;z, zxb ,; zxb ,; zxb ,;
six mix; ox fox; box bog; big bid bit; exit, exam
fizz buzz, zinc zone, hazy lazy blaze, doze dozen
```

SKILL BUILDING. These sentences stress the new strokes. They also include every stroke you have previously learned.

```
The six big, lazy boys got a dozen exam problems.
When the blaze got big, six boys ran for an exit.
Maybe the bog is afire; its zone has a big blaze.
If the six lazy boys do doze a bit, buzz quickly.
Examine the big box; then bid for six or a dozen.
If the blaze is big, mix in the six tons of zinc.
That lazy fox may doze; if so, just move his box.
```

PROBLEM 4. Type the following bulletin-board announcement with double spacing on a half sheet of paper. Leave one extra blank line space below the heading. Plan the vertical and horizontal centering carefully before you start.

Make the display heading with the $-sign. Type straight across the page—line for line. Do not make the letters individually.

Use a six-inch line for the body of the announcement.

Note: The entire alphabet is shown in display letters at the bottom of this page. The letter *I*, you will notice, is the only letter that is not five spaces wide. When you type a heading that contains one or more *I*'s, be sure to make the proper adjustment in your calculations for horizontal centering. If your display heading contains more than one word, leave five spaces between words.

Commercial Club dues must be paid by December 9. The

Treasurer, Claude Carlton, will be in Room 487 each day this

week during the noon free period, 12:30 to 1:15. If you are

planning to attend the Commercial Club Christmas party, make

sure that your dues are paid in full.

James Bellingham, President

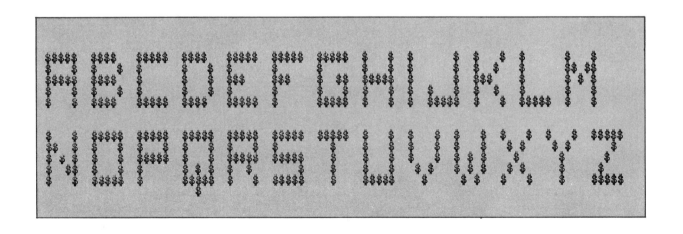

WORD DRILL. Each line of words contains a high-frequency letter combination that includes one of the new strokes.

bore born borne borax labor arbor harbor neighbor
expel expand expanse expose export expend explain
ban band bandy bandit bank banker bankrupt banish
size prize; civilize utilize; authorize organize;
rob robe probe problem throb job mob mobile globe
exist, existence, exhaust, exhibit, exhort, exile

SENTENCE WRITING. These sentences use many of the words you just practiced. Remember: If your arms feel strained, you are probably sitting too close to your typewriter.

Mobile labor does exist; organize and utilize it.
This exhibit shows how a bandit may rob the bank.
Authorize the banker to expose the labor problem.
Size is a problem; a harbor must expand to exist.
An exhibit helps our neighbor to explain his job.
The banker is bankrupt, out of job, and in exile.
———1———2———3———4———5———6———7———8———9———

PARAGRAPH PREVIEW. Your goal with these words is stroking mastery. Accuracy on them will increase your speed on the paragraph that follows.

good skill keep feet floor you are in be on typed
your posture required realize learning stationary

PARAGRAPH TYPING. *Move the line space lever to 2.* This paragraph contains all the letters of the alphabet. Type it line for line.

	Words
You must realize, of course, that good posture is	10
one of the various factors which are vital in the	20
job of learning how to build typing skill. It is	30
important you make sure your body does not sag if	40
you lean forward to study the copy required to be	50
typed. Keep your feet flat on the floor and your	60
hands and arms almost stationary; relax and type.	70

———1———2———3———4———5———6———7———8———9———

UNDERSCORING AND SPREADING TITLES. When you want to make a long heading or a long title stand out on the sheet, you will usually get the effect you want simply by underscoring the words. When the title is fairly short, on the other hand, you should spread the title by leaving extra spaces between the letters and the words.

Spread a title by leaving one space after each letter and three spaces after each word.

TAX LAW MADE EASY

Tax Law Made Easy

T A X   L A W   M A D E   E A S Y

T a x   L a w   M a d e   E a s y

Sometimes a title looks best when it is both spread and underscored. The underscoring may extend under the spread-out word, or it may be confined to the individual letters.

T A X   L A W   M A D E   E A S Y

T a x   L a w   M a d e   E a s y

T A X   L A W   M A D E   E A S Y

T a x   L a w   M a d e   E a s y

TYPING TITLE PAGES. A title page offers many opportunities for you to use your own taste in arrangement. There are, however, two basic principles that you should follow.

1. Make the space between the top of the sheet and the title the same as the space between the last line and the bottom of the sheet.

2. Type the author's name considerably closer to the title than to the lines at the bottom of the page.

Look again at the illustration on the preceding page to see how these principles have been applied.

PROBLEM 2. Type a title page from the copy given below. Use the sheet on which you typed a border in Problem 1.

Type the title 2½ inches from the top edge of the sheet (1½ inches below the border). Spread the title and type it in all capitals.

Type the word *by* one inch below the title.

Double-space each of the two-line groups. Use the current year date.

TAX LAW MADE EASY

by
Charles Rosewall

New York City
19—

PROBLEM 3. Use the copy given below to prepare a title page. Make a border by using either the small *x*, the asterisk, or the period—whichever you prefer.

Spread the title and type it in all capitals. Underscore the words in the title.

Use the current year date.

THE STORY OF POLO

by
David Jennings

South Bend, Indiana
19—

DISPLAY LETTERS. There are several ways to make large display letters on the typewriter. One of the most legible styles—and one that you will find easy to use—is illustrated in the following heading.

Note that each display letter contains five vertical strokes and five horizontal strokes. There are two spaces between letters.

To center horizontally a word typed in display letters, simply find the number of horizontal spaces in the word and proceed as usual. The four letters in the word *DUES*, for example, occupy 20 spaces (4 x 5), and there are 6 spaces between letters (3 x 2)—a total of 26 horizontal spaces.

LESSON 7
Timed Typing

Line length for this lesson—50 spaces. Set the left margin stop. Set the line space lever at 1. In this lesson you will get practice in indenting. Read the instructions for setting a tabulator stop; then set a stop for indenting the paragraphs of this lesson.

SETTING A TABULATOR STOP. The first line of each paragraph you will type in this lesson is indented 5 spaces. To make that indention, set a tabulator stop 5 spaces in from the left margin.

First remove all stops that may now be set. Move the carriage all the way across while you hold down the tabulator clear key.

After all stops have been cleared, simply (1) move the carriage to the point at which you want to set a tabulator stop and (2) press the tabulator set key. The carriage will then jump from the left margin to that point whenever you hold down the tabulator key or bar.

PREVIEW PRACTICE. Type each of the following lines twice. Double-space after each two-line group. The words are selected from the Continuous Typing paragraphs. Concentrate on accurate stroking.

even get use desire going typing watching nothing
you great will skill tell strike strokes progress
be between degree apply attained regular increase

CONTINUOUS TYPING. *Move the line space lever to 2.* Type these paragraphs line for line. Omit the numbers. Be sure to indent.

Words

1

	Words
When watching anyone who can type with great	9
speed, you will note that he or she taps the keys	19
with an even tempo; if it is your desire to reach	29
a high degree of skill, you must apply that habit	39
to your own work. You should learn to strike the	49
keys in such a way that your time between strokes	59
is about equal; increase this tempo when you can.	69

—1—2—3—4—5—6—7—8—9—

2

		Words
Nothing is more vital to regular progress in	9	78
the field of typing than plenty of the right kind	19	88
of practice; your goal cannot be attained without	29	98
it. Persons who have made a study of how to form	39	108
habits tell us that you may get much benefit from	49	118
going back later to some of the material that you	59	128
typed before and typing it again. Use that hint.	69	138

—1—2—3—4—5—6—7—8—9—

WARM-UP   Pay them for the work if they aid us to dismantle the span.

ALPHABET   His growing firms exported quaint black jars of every size.

CONTROL   Larry sells immense kettles of copper and corrugated steel.

TYPING BORDERS. You will often want to "dress up" a page of typed material by including a border. Note how the border improves the appearance of the title page shown at the right.

These practical suggestions will help you to type borders easily and neatly.

1. Keep the design simple. The best characters to use are the small *o*, the small *x*, the period, and the asterisk.

The title page illustrated at the right has a border made with the small *o*. The designs below show other effects that you can get.

```
x x x x x      . . . . .      * * * * *
x                  .              *
x                  .              *
x                  .              *
x                  .              *
x                  .              *
```

2. Use 1-inch margins all around the sheet. Although other margins are sometimes used, the standard 1-inch margin is easiest to plan.

Put a pencil mark one inch from the bottom of the sheet before you insert the sheet in your machine. That mark will tell you where to type the bottom line of the border. Space down seven lines from the top of the sheet for the top line.

3. In typing the top and bottom lines of the border, type only on *alternate* spaces.

4. For greatest precision, type the vertical lines (the two sides of the border) by typing *across* the sheet. Set the line space regulator for single spacing. Set a margin stop one inch from the left edge and a tabulator stop one inch from the right edge.

5. To reduce the jar on your machine, set another tabulator stop about half way across the page. On each line of writing, you will then (a) strike the key for the left line, (b) strike the tabulator key *twice*, and (c) strike the key for the right line.

PROBLEM 1. Using the small letter *o*, type a border on an 8½ by 11 sheet. Follow the suggestions which you have just studied.

When you have finished, keep your work for use in completing a title page in Problem 2.

Speed Building

Set the line space lever at 1. Type twice each line of Word Drill, Sentence Writing, and Paragraph Preview. Double-space after each two-line group.

WORD DRILL. Each line is made up of words that contain the same high-frequency letter combination. Learn to type by letter groups for speed!

```
casual usual visual actual ritual manual equality
sighted united visited cited voted routed invited
national relation action auction suction solution
prevail previous prestige prefix predict precious
pores port porch porous export report spore sport
form formal forms formula forgive fortune conform
```

SENTENCE WRITING. These sentences are designed for speed. They contain many of the words you just practiced. Type them at your best rate.

```
Formal action united the national port directors.
She invited previous national chairmen to report.
He cited the usual relation to national prestige.
He pores over an actual formula for the solution.
They visited the auction and invited formal bids.
She voted to conform to the ritual of the manual.
```
———1———2———3———4———5———6———7———8———9———

PARAGRAPH PREVIEW. This practice gives you a chance to master the fingering of special words selected from the paragraph that follows.

```
way are be on your higher energy utilize practice
expect best avoid useless bouncing bearing typing
```

PARAGRAPH TYPING. *Move the line space lever to 2. Set a tab stop for a 5-space indention.* This paragraph contains all letters of the alphabet. Type it line for line.

	Words
One way to get higher speed and to gain more	9
skill is to make serious efforts to avoid useless	19
motions; you cannot expect best results if you do	29
not utilize your energy solely in those ways that	39
have a bearing on your job. The poor practice of	49
bouncing your hands and arms while you are typing	59
must be avoided; take firm steps to conquer it.	68

———1———2———3———4———5———6———7———8———9———

TYPING POETRY. A poem that consists of more than one stanza should be typed with single spacing, with double spacing between stanzas.

Center the poem on the sheet.

When the author's name appears below the poem, type that name to end under the last stroke of the longest line. Always double-space between the last line of the poem and the author's name.

Certain lines of a poem are often indented. Set a tabulator stop in advance for those lines. The usual indention is three spaces.

PROBLEM 2. Type the following poem on an 8½ by 11 sheet of paper. Leave *two* blank lines between the heading and the first line of the poem.

Set a left margin of 23 pica spaces or 32 elite spaces. When you make your calculations for vertical centering, provide for the blank lines.

The Joy of Work

I would but do my work today,
　However small it seems to be.
I can not see the distant way
　Or know what lies ahead for me.
I ask that I may never shirk,
　But rather do with right good will
Whatever task becomes my work,
　And thus my destiny fulfill.
I care not where that work is done —
　In office, home or school or store.
Be sure an inner glow is won
　By him who does his daily chore.
Who finds his work is blest indeed.
He has a joy, a happiness
Because his work supplies a need —
　The truest measure of success.

— Charles G. Reigner

LESSON 8
3 4 7 8

Line length for this lesson—50 spaces. Set the left margin stop. Set the line space lever at 1 until you are told to move it. Type each line on this page twice with single spacing. Double-space after each two-line group.

WARM-UP REVIEW. These sentences review all the letters of the alphabet and all the punctuation marks you have now learned.

```
When the pen broke, the lazy man tried to fix it.
Janet came quickly; she drove both day and night.
```

TRAINING YOUR FINGERS. To strike any key on the top row, extend your finger until it is nearly straight. Your arm will move forward slightly as you make the reach. Remember, however, that the principal motion should always be the forward movement of your *finger*.

"Get the feel" of the new keys by watching the keyboard while you make the reaches a few times. Then *look away from the keyboard* and "shadow-type" **34** *space* **78** *space* for several moments.

Left Hand
3—Use D finger
4—Use F finger

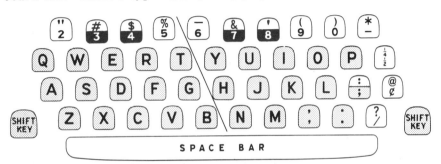

Right Hand
7—Use J finger
8—Use K finger

KEY LOCATION PRACTICE. The words included in these lines will help you associate top-row keys with home-row keys.

```
34 78 34 78 347 348 34 78 783 784 378 384 748 473
ode 33 ride 383 tide 373 jut 77 jury 737 just 747
fry 44 fray 484 frog 474 ski 88 skid 838 skit 848
```

SKILL BUILDING. These sentences provide applied practice on the new keys. They include all the letters of the alphabet, the period, the comma, and the semicolon.

```
Add 4 to 74 to get 78.  Add 34 to 43; you get 77.
Take 44 from 88 and then add 33; you must get 77.
If 34 plus 7 plus 3 is 44, 74 plus 7 and 3 is 84.
Divide 348 by 4; remember that 348 is 4 times 87.
Joe may require us to exclude 37 or 38 zinc bins.
When it makes 748 turns, the marker shows 77,748.
Make 73 or 74 cakes; she sold tickets to 838 men.
```

Double-space #

MINUTES
Regular Monthly Meeting

Phoenix Camera Club
March 20, 19--

The regular monthly meeting of the Phoenix Camera
Club was held in the club's meeting room in Ramsay Hall
on Wednesday evening, March 20, 19--. President Dawson
presided. There were 26 members and guests present.   *2*
¶ The minutes of the February meeting were read and ap-
proved as read.

The Treasurer reported receipts of $15.50 and dis-
bursements of $9.78, leaving a balance of $43.12.

l.c. The Secretary read a letter from the President of
The Westview Camera Society, thanking us for our hospi-
tality at our "Fellowship Meeting" in February.

Marjorie Street, Chairman of the Annual Exhibit   *of 75¢*
Committee, reported that an exhibit fee will be charged
each member who exhibits this year, the fee to cover the
stet rental cost of display materials and equipment.

-- if possible --
Malcolm Foster moved, seconded by Beatrice O'hara,
that the meeting night be changed from the third Wednesday to the first Wednesday of each month, the change
to become effective in September. The motion was carried by a voice vote. after a short discussion. ¶

No ¶ President Dawson instructed the Chairman of the
Housing Committee, Robert Bollinger, to try to make the
necessary arrangements with the management of Ramsay
Hall and to report at our next meeting.

The meeting was adjourned at 9:05 p. m., after
which Clarence Robinson, Chairman of the Program Committee, introduced Dr. Claude J. Webber, who gave us a
delightful talk on "Getting the Light Right."

#
Respectfully Submitted,
l.c.

Florence D. Astor, Secretary

Speed Building

Type twice each line of Word Drill, Sentence Writing, and Paragraph Preview. Double-space after each two-line group.

WORD DRILL. Continue to build your speed by mastering letter combinations that come up with high frequency in all copy. Type by letter groups!

```
dish fish wish swish relish finish varnish banish
one none done throne honest lone alone tone stone
hose chose those arose prose dose nose close pose
tent content extent dent indent lent enter center
cent scent vent event bent sent absent spent went
slice splice advice device nice spice twice price
```

SENTENCE WRITING. Now apply your speed to the same letter combinations. Each of these sentences contains several of the words you just practiced.

```
They do relish the tone and content of his prose.
His honest advice is to varnish this chair twice.
Alice chose this candy and spent one cent for it.
Those men sent enough stone to finish the throne.
The price of one fish dish on the menu went down.
Use this device to splice the center of the tent.
———1———2———3———4———5———6———7———8———9———
```

PARAGRAPH PREVIEW. Type these more difficult words the first time for mastery; then try to pick up speed on the second writing.

```
since after each avoid lazy throw throws required
by page you typing minute speed carriage snappily
```

PARAGRAPH TYPING. *Move the line space lever to 2. Set a stop for a 5-space indention.* Type this paragraph line for line. It contains all letters of the alphabet.

	Words
Since you throw the carriage after each line	9
typed, just one second lost each time that you do	19
so extends by one minute the typing time required	29
for each page with single spacing. To help avoid	39
losing time, throw the carriage snappily; you cut	49
down speed when you make lazy carriage throws.	58

———1———2———3———4———5———6———7———8———9———

WARM-UP They paid the man to fix the giant sign and the big signal.

ALPHABET The quiet experts have just drawn big prizes for lucky men.

CONTROL Three happy college roommates will soon meet our professor.

Copy in longhand or typewritten copy with longhand corrections is called "rough draft." This Practice Unit will give you training and experience in typing from rough draft copy.

CORRECTION SYMBOLS. Certain symbols for indicating corrections have come into general use. The most widely used symbols are illustrated and explained in the list on this page. Study that list carefully. The examples are taken from the minutes that you will type in Problem 1.

TYPING MINUTES OF A MEETING. The minutes for a club or for any other organization may be typed in a number of acceptable ways. The exact form is frequently set by custom or by the kind of book in which the minutes are kept.

The important thing to remember is that the first draft of the minutes should be so arranged that there is room for corrections and additions. Use double spacing and provide ample margins.

PROBLEM 1. The minutes of a club meeting are shown in rough draft form on the next page. Type them in final form. You will need two sheets of 8½ by 11 paper.

Leave a top margin of 2 inches on the first page and 1½ inches on the second page. Set stops for left and right margins of 1½ inches each. The bottom margin of the first page should be between 1 and 1½ inches.

Leave two blank line spaces between the heading and the first line of the minutes.

Symbol	Meaning	Example
¶	Start a new paragraph here.	¶The minutes of the
no ¶	Do not make a paragraph here.	no ¶President Dawson instructed
#	Leave space here; open up.	MINUTES #
◡	Remove space here; close up.	Regular Monthly Meeting
≡	Change small letter to a capital.	9:05 p. m.
l.c.	Change capital to a small (lower case) letter.	by Beatrice O'hara
∿	Transpose the letters.	l.c. The Westview Camera Society
⌣	Transpose the words.	Feburary meeting
[	Move to the left to this point.	Dr. Claude J. Webber
]	Move to the right to this point.	[Florence D. Astor
∧	Insert material here.	Malcolm Foster
ϑ	Omit crossed out material; delete.	fee will be charged of 75¢
stet	Keep as originally written; disregard mark to delete.	vote. after a short discussion. stet rental cost of display

78   **PRACTICE UNIT 15**

LESSON 9
5 6 9 0

Line length for this lesson—50 spaces. Set the left margin stop. Set the line space lever at 1 until you are told to change the setting. Type each line on this page twice with single spacing. Double-space after each two-line group.

WARM-UP REVIEW. These sentences include all the letters of the alphabet plus all the other strokes you have now learned.

Paul may come next month; his road is now frozen.

Vivian did buy 374 quaint jugs, but she broke 48.

TRAINING YOUR FINGERS. In making any of the long reaches to the top row, you will normally lift more than one finger. When you make the long reach to *6*, for example, let your fingers spread fanwise, but keep the little finger anchored in home position.

While you look at the keyboard, practice the new reaches a few times without striking the keys. Then look away from the keyboard and "shadow-type" 5 *space* 690 *space*. Practice until you can make each reach automatically.

Left Hand
5—Use F finger

Right Hand
6—Use J finger
9—Use L finger
0—Use ; finger

KEY LOCATION PRACTICE. When you strike the *9*, keep home position with either your first finger or your fourth finger—whichever seems easier for you.

5 690 5 690 569 560 5 690 956 950 605 609 590 906

aft 55 left 505 loft 595 shy 66 gushy 606 why 696

solo 99 silo 959 log 969 hop 00 shop 050 stop 060

SKILL BUILDING. Each of these sentences uses the new strokes. The entire group also reviews all the other strokes you have learned so far.

Divide 3 into 90; you get 30, which is 5 times 6.

Add 30 to 30 to make 60; then add 30 more for 90.

Now question 8 or 9 of the 750 men and 940 women.

Note how 55 is 5 more than 50 and 5 less than 60.

They expect 680, but 64 or 65 more may join them.

He sold 5,640 at 96 cents a dozen and kept 5,960.

The stock went from 97 to 99 and then down to 96.

The illustration on this page shows a second way in which outlines are sometimes typed. Notice especially that the title of each main division is typed in solid capital letters. There is a blank line space below that title and another blank line space at the end of the division. The rest of the outline is typed with single spacing.

It is all right to space just once—rather than twice—after the period that follows a number or letter in an outline if you do so consistently.

PROBLEM 2. Type this outline in the style illustrated on this page. Use a 1½-inch left margin if your machine has pica type and a 2-inch left margin if your machine has elite type.

Set tabulator stops at 5-space intervals. Base the first indention on the Roman numeral III.

Center the heading on line 17 from the top edge of the sheet. Triple-space after the heading.

In typing this outline, leave *one* space after each period.

```
                    STAMP COLLECTING AS A HOBBY

        I. HOW TO START A COLLECTION
             A. Supplies needed
                  1. Album
                  2. Hinges
                  3. Magnifier
                  4. Watermark detector
             B. Stamp sources
                  1. Old correspondence
                  2. Stamp dealers
                       a. Listed in classified telephone book
                       b. Advertise in some magazines
                  3. Exchanges
       II. STAMP CLUBS
             A. Membership
             B. Activities
                  1. "Treasure hunt"
                  2. "Auction sale"
                  3. Stamp trading
      III. HOW TO SPECIALIZE
             A. According to country
             B. According to subject
             C. Commemoratives
             D. Plate-number blocks
             E. First-day covers
```

STAMP COLLECTING AS A HOBBY

I. HOW TO START A COLLECTION

A. Supplies needed
    1. Album
    2. Hinges
    3. Magnifier
    4. Watermark detector
B. Stamp sources
    1. Old correspondence
    2. Stamp dealers
        a. Listed in classified telephone books
        b. Advertise in some magazines
    3. Exchanges

II. STAMP CLUBS

A. Membership
B. Activities
    1. "Treasure hunt"
    2. "Auction sale"
    3. Stamp trading

III. HOW TO SPECIALIZE

A. According to country
B. According to subject
C. Commemoratives
D. Plate-number blocks
E. First-day covers

Speed Building

Type each line of Word Drill, Sentence Writing, and Paragraph Preview twice with single spacing. Double-space after each two-line group.

WORD DRILL. These lines will help you to build speed by mastering additional letter combinations that appear with high frequency in familiar words.

```
thick thicket stick ticket brick trick sick quick
ride bride pride side beside preside inside glide
stride wide hide tide guide provide divide decide
rink drink brink shrink trinket blink pink thinks
lock block clock flock rock stock mock shock dock
mystify testify gratify signify specify diversify
```

SENTENCE WRITING. These sentences, which include many of the words you just practiced, are designed for fast writing. Try to type them at your top speed.

```
Lock the pink ticket inside the clock to hide it.
Any quick shock makes our guide blink and shrink.
She thinks he may decide to testify for her side.
Ride down that block to gratify their sick guide.
The brink of the wide rock is beside the thicket.
Specify how much brick and thick rock to provide.
```
—— 1 —— 2 —— 3 —— 4 —— 5 —— 6 —— 7 —— 8 —— 9 ——

PARAGRAPH PREVIEW. Your practice on these selected words will increase the speed and accuracy with which you type the paragraph that follows.

```
speed good yourself in stages as exert vital hope
initial realize factor later turning jobs rapidly
```

PARAGRAPH TYPING. *Move the line space lever to 2. Set a stop for a 5-space indention.* Type this paragraph line for line. It contains all the letters of the alphabet.

	Words
Each habit you develop in the initial stages	9
of your work readily emerges as a vital factor in	19
the quality of the work that you may do later and	29
in the speed with which you can do that work. If	39
you hope to realize your goal of turning out good	49
jobs rapidly, exert yourself to form good habits.	59

—— 1 —— 2 —— 3 —— 4 —— 5 —— 6 —— 7 —— 8 —— 9 ——

WARM-UP   Eight sorority girls may enamel the six big emblems for us.

ALPHABET   Two bald typing wizards have quickly justified six margins.

CONTROL   The Alton Kane Company got control of Yen Brothers of Troy.

Your first step in typing an outline is to set equally spaced tabulator stops for the subdivisions. Base the first indention on the *longest* Roman numeral. In the outline shown on this page, for example, the numeral II starts at the margin. The numeral I is indented one space.

PROBLEM 1. Type this outline with double spacing. Space twice after each period and after each set of parentheses.

Set a 1-inch left margin for a pica machine or a 1½-inch left margin for an elite machine. Set tabulator stops at 5-space intervals.

Center the heading on the twelfth line from the top edge of the sheet. Leave one *extra* line space below the heading.

```
                     GUIDE FOR TYPING OUTLINES

        I.  Division designations
            A.  Roman numerals for main divisions
            B.  Capital letters for major subdivisions
            C.  Arabic numbers and small letters for minor subdivisions
                1.  Numbers and letters alternated throughout outline
                2.  Parentheses and underscores used when necessary
                    a.  Parentheses
                        (1)  Accompany second use of Arabic numbers
                        (2)  Accompany second use of small letters
                    b.  Underscores
                        (1)  Accompany third use of Arabic numbers
                        (2)  Accompany third use of small letters
                        (3)  Seen only in certain outlines
                            (a)  Rarely needed
                            (b)  Preferably avoided
        II. Spacing and indentions
            A.  Double spacing preferred
```

GUIDE FOR TYPING OUTLINES

I. Division designations
  A. Roman numerals for main divisions
  B. Capital letters for major subdivisions
  C. Arabic numbers and small letters for minor subdivisions
    1. Numbers and letters alternated throughout outline
    2. Parentheses and underscores used when necessary
      a. Parentheses
        (1) Accompany second use of Arabic numbers
        (2) Accompany second use of small letters
      b. Underscores
        (1) Accompany third use of Arabic numbers
        (2) Accompany third use of small letters
        (3) Seen only in certain outlines
          (a) Rarely needed
          (b) Preferably avoided
II. Spacing and indentions
  A. Double spacing preferred
  B. Extra line space after heading
  C. Uniform spacing after period
  D. Five-space indentions preferred

LESSON 10

Timed Typing

Line length for this lesson—50 spaces. Set the left margin stop. Set a stop for a 5-space indention. Set the line space lever at 1. The words in the Preview Practice have been selected from the paragraphs you will type. Concentrate on your stroking of those words.

PREVIEW PRACTICE. Type each line of words twice. Try to pick up speed on the second writing. Double-space after each two-line group.

```
manner errors quickness bottom all fall corrected
will still carriage art moving hazardous mistakes
we area up erase seven forward acquire confidence
near neat zeal use six matches importance lightly
```

CONTINUOUS TYPING. *Move the line space lever to 2 for double spacing.* Type these paragraphs line for line. Omit the numbers. Each paragraph contains all the letters of the alphabet.

Words

1

```
     Excel in the art of making an erasure so the       9
correction will not likely be noticed.  While all      19
of us make some mistakes, the manner in which the      29
errors are corrected is of major importance.  You      39
must be able to make an erasure with so much zeal      49
and positive confidence that it will be done with      59
quickness and still produce neat and clean work.       69
——1——2——3——4——5——6——7——8——9——
```

2

```
     First we must prepare to erase by moving the       9    78
carriage all the way to the left or to the right,      19    88
since grit and paper particles that fall into the      29    98
machine basket can be hazardous.  Raise the paper      39   108
bail and turn up your paper six or seven lines to      49   118
make the mistake simple to correct.  Just be sure      59   128
your eraser is clean; acquire and use a shield.        69   138
——1——2——3——4——5——6——7——8——9——
```

3

```
     Expect a change in procedure if the area you        9   147
have to erase is near the bottom of the page; the      19   157
typist then turns the paper down from the top and      29   167
brings the bottom forward to erase and so reduces      39   177
the hazard of getting the paper out of alignment.      49   187
Then just strike the right keys lightly until the      59   197
retyped shade matches or equals the original.         68   206
——1——2——3——4——5——6——7——8——9——
```

TYPING INVOICES. When you study the invoice shown at the right, you will see that it is considerably more detailed than the bills you have just typed.

Notice especially that one tabulator stop often takes care of several different parts of the invoice.

Note, too, that the typing is centered in the four columns that contain figures. The items in the *Description* column, on the other hand, are blocked two spaces from the left edge of the column.

LARKIN'S
INCORPORATED

2463 NORTH STATE STREET
EVANSVILLE, INDIANA 47704

Invoice No. D-1001

Jarman's Sport Shop
188 Fifth Avenue
Galveston, Texas 77550

Invoice Date April 27, 19--

Terms: Net 30 Days

Your Order No. 468		How Shipped Crawford Fast Freight	Date Shipped 4/27/--	
QUANTITY	STOCK NO.	DESCRIPTION	UNIT PRICE	TOTAL
12	M-592	"Zero" Portable Ice Chest	10.80	129.60
4	R-26	Two-burner Camp Stove	7.55	30.20
1	R-27	"Master Chef" Camp Stove	14.30	14.30
				174.10
		Prepaid freight charges		5.45
				179.55

PROBLEM 3. Type the following invoice on Form 13-3. It is the same invoice illustrated above. Follow the illustration as a model for arranging your work. Use the current year in all dates.

Jarman's Sport Shop
188 Fifth Avenue
Galveston, Texas 77550

Invoice No. **D-1001**
Invoice Date **April 27, 19—**

Your Order No. **468**		*How Shipped* **Crawford Fast Freight**	*Date Shipped* **4/27/—**	
Quantity	*Stock No.*	*Description*	*Unit Price*	*Total*
12	M-592	"Zero" Portable Ice Chest	10.80	129.60
4	R-26	Two-burner Camp Stove	7.55	30.20
1	R-27	"Master Chef" Camp Stove	14.30	14.30
				174.10
		Prepaid freight charges		5.45
				179.55

PROBLEM 4. Type this invoice on Form 13-4. Use this year in all dates.

Walbert & Grason, Inc.
Main and Center Streets
Jackson, Mississippi 39202

Invoice No. **D-1002**
Invoice Date **April 27, 19—**

Your Order No. **K-502**		*How Shipped* **Parcel Post**	*Date Shipped* **4/27/—**	
Quantity	*Stock No.*	*Description*	*Unit Price*	*Total*
48	C-1030	"Outdoor Living" Utensil Set	1.75	84.00
24	T-929	Picnic Table Cover (red)	2.05	49.20
24	T-930	Picnic Table Cover (green)	2.05	49.20
				182.40
		Parcel post charges		4.82
				187.22

75

Speed Building

Set the line space lever at 1. Type twice each line of Word Drill, Sentence Writing, and Paragraph Preview. Double-space after each two-line group.

WORD DRILL. You will feel your speed shoot up on these lines. All words in each line contain the same high-frequency letter combination.

```
old bold cold scold fold gold hold mold sold told
long along belong strong throng wrong song tongue
trust rust crust dust gust just adjust must joust
back lack black slack snack pack track sack stack
bale gale male pale sale inhale whale shale stale
lain plain brain grain train gain chain main pain
```

SENTENCE WRITING. These fast sentences include many of the words you just practiced. Push for your top speed—especially on the second writing of each line.

```
She sold an old gold chain that did belong to me.
He told them they must inhale dust and stale air.
Just one old train runs along the main track now.
She must fold back the long black hem to pack it.
The old chain did hold the stack during the gale.
He just sold their sack of grain and bale of hay.
```
——1——2——3——4——5——6——7——8——9——

PARAGRAPH PREVIEW. Concentrate as you type these words. If the first typing of a line seems "ragged," try to smooth out your stroking on the second writing.

```
progress possibly three need weeks be no not rate
jump realize morale typing expect overnight raise
```

PARAGRAPH TYPING. *Set the line space lever at 2. Set a stop for a 5-space indention.* Type the paragraph line for line. It contains the entire alphabet.

Words

```
      It is of value to your morale to realize the      9
progress you make may not be regular and that you      19
can expect days when there is almost no change in      29
your typing rate.  You may possibly jump three or      39
more words almost overnight and yet require three      49
or more weeks to raise your typing rate again.         58
```
——1——2——3——4——5——6——7——8——9——

WARM-UP   The apt man may fix the oak chair and enamel it with ivory.

ALPHABET   Jack quoted my price for the dozen vacant duplex bungalows.

CONTROL   Mary Jane may tour Kentucky and Ohio if she visits Indiana.

TYPING BILLS. The typical bill is typed on a small two-part form. The date of the bill and the name and address of the debtor are typed in the upper part of the form. The lower part is used for a brief description of the service rendered and for the amount of the charge.

For best appearance make the left and right margins equal and type the date to end at the right margin. If the bill is to be mailed in a window envelope, be sure to place the debtor's name and address where they will show through the window.

The bill shown below is the one that you will type in your first problem. Study it carefully.

FRANK LANGLEY MOORE
Certified Public Accountant
33 WEST TENTH STREET
ATLANTIC CITY, N.J. 08402

April 1, 19--

The Fashion Shop
2046 Ocean Avenue
Atlantic City, New Jersey 08401

FOR PROFESSIONAL SERVICES:

March 15 tax return $25.00
Statement for first quarter   15.00
                               $40.00

PROBLEM 1. Type this bill with one-inch left and right margins. The date goes on the second line below the heading, and the address starts on line 14 from the top. Leave three blank line spaces below *FOR PROFESSIONAL SERVICES.* Type the items on the bill with double spacing.

Use Form 13-1. Date the bill today.

The Fashion Shop
2046 Ocean Avenue
Atlantic City, New Jersey   08401

March 15 tax return	**$25.00**
Statement for first quarter	**15.00**
	$40.00

PROBLEM 2. Type this bill on Form 13-2. Set one-inch left and right margins.

The illustration below shows how the bill should look. The date is typed two line spaces below the heading, and the debtor's name is typed on the 14th line from the top edge. There are two blank spaces below the double rule.

Warren J. Cooper & Sons
Charlottesville, Virginia 22901

September 8, 19--

Mr. Gregory D. Francis, Jr.
78 North Wilson Road
Charlottesville, Virginia 22903

TERMS: Net Cash

Installation of flagstone walk and repairs to porch
steps of residence $173.90

Type a leader (periods on alternate spaces) from the end of the explanation. Stop the leader a few spaces before the dollar mark. Use today's date.

Mr. Gregory D. Francis, Jr.
78 North Wilson Road
Charlottesville, Virginia   22903

Installation of flagstone walk and repairs to porch steps of residence........$173.90

LESSON 11

2 - 1 ?

Line length for this lesson—50 spaces. Set the left margin stop. Set the line space lever at 1 until you are told to move it. Type each line on this page twice with single spacing. Double-space after each two-line group.

WARM-UP REVIEW. These sentences include all the keys you have now learned—including the number keys covered in earlier lessons.

```
He required just 75 minutes to cover 60 problems.
Franz got 48 or 49 keys; now fix 37 more, please.
```

TRAINING YOUR FINGERS. Locate the new keys. Note that the ? is a shift character. To type the ?, you will hold down the left shift key with your left little finger while you strike the key with your right little finger. Keep your first finger anchored in home position.

Try the new reaches while you look at the keyboard. Then look away from the keyboard and "shadow-type" **2** *space* **–1?** *space* for several moments.

Left Hand
2—Use S finger
1—Use A finger when there is a key for 1 on the top row

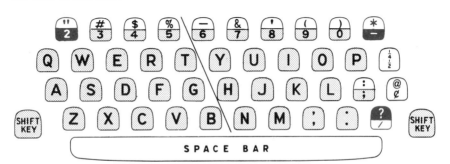

Right Hand
– —Use ; finger
1 —Small L
? —(Shift) Use ; finger

KEY LOCATION PRACTICE. Remember to depress the left shift key *all the way* before you strike the ? and to *hold it down until you have made the stroke.*

```
2 -1? 2 -1? 2 -1? 1- 2? 2 -1? 2 -1? 2- 21? 12 1-2
swig 22 swish 2- swipe 12 rap -- lap -2- help -21
tip ??? rip -2 gulp -?- sip 2?? plow 1-2 glow 211
```

SKILL BUILDING. Note the periods in the third sentence. Space *once* —not twice—after a period that follows an abbreviation within a sentence.

```
If 22 and 2 make 24, how much is 20 plus 2 and 2?
Is the 1812-1822 period mentioned on pages 21-32?
Does the 12-lb. size replace the old 15-lb. size?
Faye may exhibit 12 jade rings; she has 21 or 22.
If 290 men are given the quiz, will 162-172 fail?
How many 250-page novels did she write--21 or 31?
Can she make the 821-mile trip in 11 or 12 hours?
```

PROBLEM 2. Type the four-column tabulation shown below. Use a sheet of plain paper. Allow 7 spaces for each intercolumn.

Triple-space after the main heading. Double-space the rest of your work.

Underscore the column headings.

To center the column heading for the first or the second column, you will space forward from the left edge of the column. The headings for the third and fourth columns are centered by backspacing.

COUNTY BASKETBALL LEAGUE

20 Leading Scorers

Player	Team	Games	Points
White	Windber	20	348
Jackson	Somerset	20	337
Olsen	Rummel	18	336
Otis	Rockwood	19	321
Stevens	Friedens	19	310
North	Windber	18	303
Brooks	Garrett	20	297
Yocum	Friedens	15	291
Reilly	Rockwood	17	290
Harper	Somerset	20	282
Linton	Salisbury	14	276
Hoover	Salisbury	16	274
Ott	Somerset	19	263
Williams	Elton	15	260
Cronin	Windber	18	258
Oakes	Garrett	17	253
Coard	Rockwood	15	252
Browne	Friedens	17	251
Adams	Windber	16	251
Tyler	Rockwood	19	250

WORD DRILL. The words in each line all contain the same 3-letter high-frequency combination. Speed up by typing the three letters as a group!

```
repair pair despair chair hair flair stair unfair
come compare compel compete comply compose income
chalk chain chaos chance change charm chart chase
shone shoe shop short shot shout shove show shown
profit promise prompt proper prove proven provide
conform inform perform reform formal normal storm
```

SENTENCE WRITING. These sentences are made up mostly of the words you just practiced. They are built for speed. Make your fingers fly!

```
That pair may prove that charm can chase despair.
It is proper to provide her the chance to comply.
To compel the shop to repair the chair is unfair.
His formal promise to come and compete is prompt.
Change the chart with chalk to show their profit.
Compare the proven profit with the normal income.
——1——2——3——4——5——6——7——8——9——
```

PARAGRAPH PREVIEW. Mastering the stroking of these words will help you to type the following paragraph more smoothly. Concentrate as you type!

```
a after attitude be bear breeze single will error
nothing through mistake realistic examine conquer
```

PARAGRAPH TYPING. *Move the line space lever to 2. Set a stop for a 5-space indention.* Type this paragraph line for line. It contains the entire alphabet.

	Words
Until you can breeze through a job of typing	9
and never make a single mistake, you will be wise	19
to adopt a realistic attitude toward errors. You	29
should bear in mind that nothing is gained if you	39
stop to examine an error when you make it; try to	49
plan to conquer errors after you finish the job.	59
——1——2——3——4——5——6——7——8——9——	

WARM-UP   An auditor may wish to amend the usual title of their form.

ALPHABET   Ben may have sold quickly six of the prize jigsaw pictures.

CONTROL   The North Magnetic Pole location is Prince of Wales Island.

The tabulation shown on this page includes a subheading (*Monthly Mileage Report of Salesmen*) and three column headings (*Month, O'Brien,* and *Lee*). The subheading, you'll notice, is centered horizontally on the sheet. The column headings, on the other hand, are centered over the columns.

When you plan horizontal placement, find the left margin setting and the tabulator settings in the usual way. The longest line in the column—not the column heading—still determines column width. To center each column heading, you will space forward or backward from the left edge of the column.

Find the difference between the number of spaces in the longest line and the number of spaces in the column heading. Divide that difference by two. The number you get is the number of spaces to indent or backspace the column heading. (Disregard a fraction.)

Look at the first column.

Spaces in longest line (September) 9
Spaces in column heading (Month) 5
                           Difference 4
Spaces to indent heading (4 ÷ 2) 2

Now look at the second column. The heading in this case is longer than the longest line.

Spaces in column heading (O'Brien) 7
Spaces in longest line (3,250) 5
                           Difference 2
Spaces to backspace heading (2 ÷ 2) 1

PROBLEM 1. Type the tabulation which is worked out for you on this page.

Triple-space after the main heading—PARAMOUNT PRODUCTS COMPANY. Double-space the rest of your work. Be sure to provide for all lines and interlines in planning vertical placement.

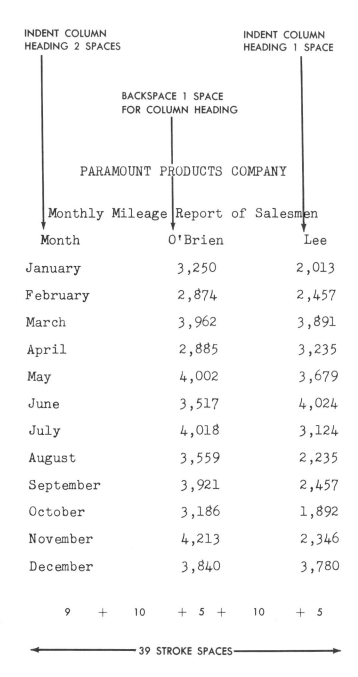

INDENT COLUMN HEADING 2 SPACES

INDENT COLUMN HEADING 1 SPACE

BACKSPACE 1 SPACE FOR COLUMN HEADING

PARAMOUNT PRODUCTS COMPANY

Monthly Mileage Report of Salesmen

Month	O'Brien	Lee
January	3,250	2,013
February	2,874	2,457
March	3,962	3,891
April	2,885	3,235
May	4,002	3,679
June	3,517	4,024
July	4,018	3,124
August	3,559	2,235
September	3,921	2,457
October	3,186	1,892
November	4,213	2,346
December	3,840	3,780

9   +   10   + 5 +   10   + 5

←—— 39 STROKE SPACES ——→

LESSON 12
The Right Margin

You have been doing all your typing line for line. When you type the Timed Typing paragraphs in this lesson, however, you will have to decide when to throw the carriage. This page will prepare you for that job. Study it carefully.

LISTENING FOR THE BELL. Your typewriter is equipped with a warning bell that is regulated by the right-hand margin setting. The carriage will lock when it reaches the margin setting; the bell, therefore, is set to ring automatically a few spaces *before* that point.

Just as soon as the bell rings, get ready to throw the carriage. If you are typing a short word, finish that word and then make the carriage throw. If you are typing a long word when the bell rings, you may have to divide that word.

Try to avoid typing more than four or five strokes after you hear the bell.

SETTING THE RIGHT MARGIN. For the paragraph work in this lesson you will need to set a right margin stop. You have already learned the proper points at which to set the left margin stop for lines of different lengths. (Refer, if necessary, to page 6 for those settings.) You can quickly set the corresponding right margin settings by simple addition.

Follow this rule for all typewriters except machines with 0 at the center of the scale.

> *To get the right margin setting, add (1) the left margin setting, (2) the number of strokes in the line you are using, and (3) the number of strokes your machine will type after the bell rings.*

For example, assume that you are going to type to a 70-stroke line, that the correct left margin setting on your machine is 8, and that your machine will type 8 spaces after the bell rings. The correct setting for the right margin is thus 8 plus 70 plus 8, or 86. The bell will ring at the end of a 70-space line (78 on the scale), but the carriage will not lock until it reaches 86.

USING THE MARGIN RELEASE KEY. If you listen for the bell on your machine, you will almost always be able to throw the carriage before it locks. In case you are using a machine that locks quite quickly after the bell rings, however, you may have to type one or two strokes beyond the margin setting to complete a word that should not be divided. The margin release key permits you to do so without changing the setting. By pressing that key, you can unlock the carriage and continue the line. The margin remains set at its original position.

WORD DIVISION. Before you start to type the paragraph work in this lesson, make yourself thoroughly familiar with the following rules for dividing a word at the end of a line.

1. Divide a word only between syllables.

The word *mistake,* for example, may be properly divided in just one way (*mis take*). A word with more than two syllables, such as *preference,* may usually be divided in more than one way (*prefer ence* or *pref erence*).

2. Never divide a one-syllable word—regardless of its length.

Such words as *thought* and *straight* are pronounced as single syllables; so, too, are certain words with *ed* endings, such as *stayed* and *fixed.*

3. Never divide a word in such a way that a single letter is typed on one line and the rest of the word is typed on another line.

Such two-syllable words as *evade, opaque,* and *pity* should not be divided.

4. Avoid dividing a word so that just two letters are carried over to the next line.

Never divide *friendly, only, ever,* or similar words. Some words, like *truthfully,* should not be divided before the final syllable, but may be properly divided elsewhere (*truth fully*).

5. When a word contains a double consonant, divide after the double letter only if that double letter is in the root word; otherwise, make the break between the two consonants.

Contrast *billing* and *pulling* (properly divided *bill ing* and *pull ing*) with *success* and *matter* (properly divided *suc cess* and *mat ter*).

6. Divide hyphenated words only at the hyphen.

7. Do not divide abbreviations, contractions, figures, or proper names.

8. Do not divide the word that comes at the end of the first line on a page.

9. Do not divide the last word on a page.

10. Try to avoid typing more than two consecutive lines that end with divided words.

WARM-UP   Their neighbor may go to the dismal island to fish for cod.

ALPHABET   Guy wants to pack six or seven dozen quart jars by himself.

CONTROL   Joseph Nelson and Sons owns New Orleans and El Paso plants.

PROBLEM 1. Type the following 3-column tabulation with single spacing. Use intercolumns of five spaces each. Double-space after the heading.

ADDRESSES AND PHONE NUMBERS OF FACULTY MEMBERS

Albert, Clifford	2168 State Street	124-5875
Bourne, Alice	327 Maple Road	837-2969
Buterbaugh, Leo	4523 Ellicott Drive	645-9401
Fitz, Robert	3912 Broadway	283-6172
Flynn, Harriet	29 Garrison Boulevard	642-5482
Haubert, Leo	1467 Eastern Parkway	837-8820
Heffner, John	15 State Street	286-3147
Jamieson, Ruth	3700 Wentworth Road	283-6009
Keller, George	673 Monroe Street	642-7808
Nicely, Marie	358 Annapolis Avenue	286-0416
Phillips, John	938 Nelson Avenue	645-4239
Quinn, Elizabeth	1705 Lake Street	124-4633
Stafford, Wilma	1846 Oliver Street	283-1163
Walker, John	915 Kentucky Avenue	837-8185
Williams, Galen	438 Harford Road	124-1683
Wilson, Ruth	4507 Vine Street	645-3551
Wolfe, Arthur	830 Summit Avenue	286-5683
Young, James	216 Belair Road	837-8149

PROBLEM 2. Type the following 4-column tabulation with double spacing. Use intercolumns of six spaces each. Triple-space after the heading.

SUGGESTED SYNONYMS FOR COMMON ADJECTIVES

cold	frigid	icy	frosty
dry	arid	rainless	waterless
fast	rapid	swift	quick
hard	difficult	tough	laborious
huge	immense	gigantic	enormous
noisy	loud	deafening	rackety
plain	clear	definite	obvious
pretty	attractive	handsome	beautiful
quiet	silent	noiseless	soundless
smooth	velvety	polished	sleek
strong	sturdy	powerful	vigorous
useful	serviceable	practicable	gainful

Timed Typing

Set margin stops for a 70-space line. Set a tab stop for a 5-space indention. Set the line space lever at 2. Type the paragraphs numbered 1, 2, and 3 as a continuous article. Omit the numbers. Your typed lines will differ from the printed lines shown here. Listen for the bell.

CORRECTING ERRORS. The paragraphs you typed in Lesson 10 gave you some hints about good erasing habits. These paragraphs contain more information about erasing. Read them before you type them.

In many offices opaque materials are used to correct errors. Such materials cover an error instead of removing it. You may use an opaque paint for this purpose; or you may hold specially coated paper over the error, then strike the same key or keys.

Words

1 The art of making an erasure so neatly and so cleanly that no one | 13
will be likely to notice a spot on the page is an art that you should | 27
take time to master.   All of us make mistakes from time to time; the | 41
thing that sets off some persons from others is the way they go about | 55
the job of remedying their mistakes.   When you do have to make an | 68
erasure, you should be able to proceed with such confidence that you | 82
will lose only a few moments and still produce work that is clean and | 96
neat. | 97

2 The first step in preparing to erase is to move the carriage all the | 14 | 111
way to the left or to the right, so that you may prevent particles of | 28 | 125
grit and paper from falling into the basket of your machine.   Lift the | 42 | 139
paper bail and then turn up the paper a few lines to put the mistake | 56 | 153
at a place where you can work in comfort.   Use a special shield if one | 70 | 167
is available and make sure that the surface of your eraser is clean. | 84 | 181
Erase with gentle strokes to keep from wearing a hole in the paper | 97 | 194
and to reduce the risk of extending the erasure over too large an area. | 112 | 209
As you erase, constantly brush away or blow away the minute bits of | 126 | 223
grit and paper; you should keep the area clean at all times. | 138 | 235

3 You should make one slight change in procedure when the spot | 12 | 247
you must erase is near the bottom of the page; the wise typist then | 26 | 261
turns the paper down from the top and brings the bottom forward | 39 | 274
for erasing to reduce the danger of getting the paper out of alignment. | 53 | 288
After you have made the erasure and have turned the paper back to | 66 | 301
do the necessary retyping, take pains to tap the correct keys with a | 80 | 315
light touch.   You want the retyped letters to match the other typing | 94 | 329
on the sheet; the only way to make sure that you get the desired result | 108 | 343
is to make faint impressions at first and then to type over the letters | 123 | 358
until the shade of the retyped letters exactly matches the original | 136 | 371
shade. | 138 | 372

Check List for Typing Tabulations

To Center Vertically . . .

✔ Count the number of lines and interlines. (Be sure to count the heading and an extra interline under the heading.)

✔ Subtract the total from 66; then divide the difference by 2 to find the line from the top edge on which to start typing.

To Center Horizontally . . .

✔ Find the total width of the tabulation (longest line in each column plus intercolumn spaces).

✔ Starting at the center of the sheet, backspace one-half the width of the tabulation; then set the left margin.

✔ Space forward the width of the first column plus the width of the intercolumn; then set a tab stop for the second column. (Continue to space forward and set stops for any additional columns.)

To Center the Heading . . .

✔ Center the sheet at the printing point.

✔ Then backspace once for every two spaces in the heading.

PROBLEM 1. Type the two-column tabulation, SOME VARIANT SPELLINGS, that has been worked out for you. Triple-space after the heading. Double-space the body of the tabulation.

PROBLEM 2. Type the following two-column tabulation with double spacing. Use an intercolumn of 10 spaces. Center the heading and type it in all capitals. Triple-space after the heading.

COMMUNICATION INVENTIONS AND INVENTORS

Fountain pen	Waterman
Linotype	Mergenthaler
Monotype	Lanston
Motion picture machine	Edison
Paper-making machine	Robert
Printing press (rotary)	Hoe
Radio broadcaster	Stubblefield
Talking machine	Edison
Telegraph	Morse
Telephone	Bell
Television	Baird
Typewriter	Sholes
Wireless	Marconi

Speed Building

Set stops for a 60-space line.   Set the line space lever at 1.   **Type each line** of words and each sentence twice.   Double-space after each **two-line group.**

WORD DRILL.   All words in each line contain the same 3-letter combination.   Learning to type that combination as a letter group will speed up your typing.

```
flag flare flakes flaky flame flap flash flashy flat flavor
float floral florist flour flout flown flows flower flowery

reality quality ability utility vanity unity charity purity
into intend intent faint paint hint mint point print sprint

able cable usable table payable capable blew visible marble
calm local vocal fiscal radical scald scalp scales calories
```

SENTENCE WRITING.   These sentences are heavily sprinkled with the words you just practiced.   Use the second writing of each line to push up your speed.

```
The local florist got his radical fiscal theory into print.

He may point out visible flakes of marble if he is capable.

The flag blew into the flame from the flare atop the float.

He did intend to paint our utility table to make it usable.

Her hint of the sum payable to charity may calm vocal foes.

Any capable florist is able to make flashy floral displays.
———1———2———3———4———5———6———7———8———9———10———11———
```

c practice

RHYTHM PRACTICE.   The drill shown at the bottom of this page is known as the *Expert's Rhythm Drill.*   It is one of the best drills for limbering up your fingers—especially at the start of a typing period.

This drill, widely used as a warm-up by professional typists, uses only the keys on the home row.

Study the pattern of the drill before you type it; then type the entire line 4 to 6 times.   After you have typed the drill a few times, you should be able to follow the pattern automatically—without referring to your book.

Caution.   To get the maximum benefit from the *Expert's Rhythm Drill*, be particularly careful to avoid bouncing your hands and arms up and down.   Train your fingers to do the work.   Learn to type this drill with a rhythmic tempo.

```
a;sldkfjghfjdksla; a;sldkfjghfjdksla; a;sldkfjghfjdksla;
```

HORIZONTAL PLACEMENT. When you get ready to type a tabulation, clear all stops from your machine. There are then just four simple steps in arranging the horizontal placement.

1. Find the width of the tabulation. A tabulation consists of columns and one or more intercolumns. The longest line in a column determines the width of that column.

Note the tabulation on this page. The width of the first column is the number of spaces in the word *catalogue*. The width of the second column is the number of spaces in the word *formulas*. The single intercolumn in this tabulation contains 10 spaces.

A quick way to find the total width is to type the separate units in a continuous line on a sheet of practice paper. Use numbers for the intercolumn spaces, thus:

```
catalogue1234567890formulas
```

Then turn to the next line and count the strokes by typing in 10's.

```
catalogue1234567890formulas
12345678901234567890123456 7
```

You now see that the width is 27 spaces.

2. Position the center of the sheet at the printing point. After you know the total width of the tabulation, you may remove the practice sheet and insert the sheet on which you are going to type the tabulation. Check the paper guide setting. Remember: You must have the printing point at the horizontal center of the *sheet*—not necessarily at the center of the scale.

3. Backspace one-half the total width of the tabulation; then set the left margin. You found the width of this tabulation, for example, to be 27 spaces. Backspace 13 spaces (27 ÷ 2 = 13½), disregarding the fraction. Set the left margin at the point where you stop backspacing.

4. Space forward to the starting point of the next column; then set a tab stop. For this tabulation, for example, space 19 spaces from the left margin—9 spaces for the word *catalogue* and 10 spaces for the intercolumn.

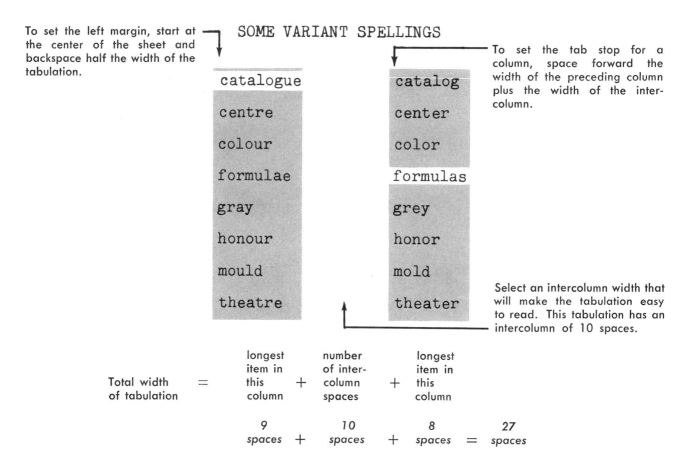

To set the left margin, start at the center of the sheet and backspace half the width of the tabulation.

SOME VARIANT SPELLINGS

To set the tab stop for a column, space forward the width of the preceding column plus the width of the intercolumn.

catalogue	catalog
centre	center
colour	color
formulae	formulas
gray	grey
honour	honor
mould	mold
theatre	theater

Select an intercolumn width that will make the tabulation easy to read. This tabulation has an intercolumn of 10 spaces.

Total width of tabulation	=	longest item in this column	+	number of intercolumn spaces	+	longest item in this column	
		9 spaces	+	10 spaces	+	8 spaces	= 27 spaces

Line length for this lesson—60 spaces. Set margin stops. Set the line space lever at 1. Type each line on this page twice with single spacing. Double-space after each two-line group.

WARM-UP REVIEW. These sentences include every stroke you have learned up to this point. Try to type the sentences evenly and accurately. Concentrate!

Go with them to the field; they must haul 78 or 79 bushels.

Did they use over 1,350 boxes to pack 640 dozen 2-qt. jars?

TRAINING YOUR FINGERS. The special characters in this lesson are shifts of the *3, 4, 7,* and *8.* Associate each character with the figure on the same key.

Without looking at the keys, "shadow-type" #$ *space* &' *space* for several moments. Be sure to practice the reach to the shift key.

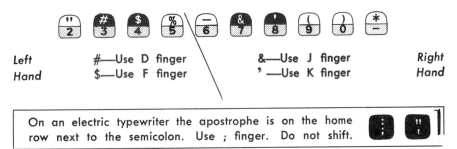

Left   #—Use D finger   &—Use J finger   Right

Hand $—Use F finger   '—Use K finger   Hand

On an electric typewriter the apostrophe is on the home row next to the semicolon. Use ; finger. Do not shift.

KEY LOCATION PRACTICE. To get the maximum benefit from your practice, shift *individually* for each of the new characters.

Erie #$ &' Judith #$ &' Frost #$ &' Kirk #$ &' Europe #$ &'

#$ &' #$ &' Elsie # Roy $ Isle ' Irish ' Ural & D#E K'I F$R

Dear Ed ## July Ur && Fred Ruhr $$ Kit Iris '' Judea &$ J&U

SKILL BUILDING. These sentences may tend to slow you down; but bear in mind that they include every stroke that you have now learned. Strive for accuracy.

She can't pay $400, and they won't settle for $300 or $350.

May Fox & O'Hanley turn down a bid for $8,390 if it's late?

He paid $175 for 156#, but he just won't pay $240 for 258#.

Which firm hasn't yet bid--O'Hara & Katz or Jones & O'Neal?

Invoices #947, #956, and #972 don't make a total of $75.31.

Lang & O'Shea won't question any bill that isn't over $150.

Check #216 is for $7.30; it's the one the bank hasn't paid.

WARM-UP   The busy tutor may aid the girl to work the prism problems.

ALPHABET   Wilma packed five dozen jars of lacquer into the gay boxes.

CONTROL   Mr. Simon Owen resigned from the Hepel Company in December.

VERTICAL PLACEMENT. You can quickly find the line on which to type the heading of any tabulation so that your work will be centered vertically on a standard 8½ x 11 sheet. Just follow this simple rule:

> *Add the number of typed lines (including the heading) to the number of interlines; subtract the total from 66; then divide by 2.*

An interline, of course, is a blank line space between typed lines. When you count the number of interlines, always allow *one more* interline below the heading than you allow below any other typed line.

Study carefully the tabulation below to see how the vertical placement is planned.

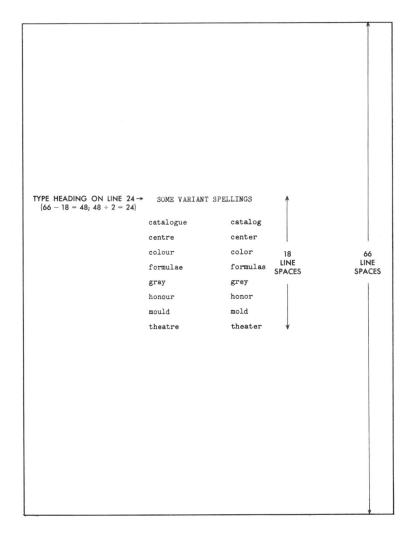

TYPE HEADING ON LINE 24 →
(66 − 18 = 48; 48 ÷ 2 = 24)

SOME VARIANT SPELLINGS

catalogue	catalog
centre	center
colour	color
formulae	formulas
gray	grey
honour	honor
mould	mold
theatre	theater

18 LINE SPACES

66 LINE SPACES

Speed Building

Type each line of Word Drill and Sentence Writing twice with **single spacing**. Double-space after each two-line group.

WORD DRILL. This practice will extend your speed-building program of typing by letter groups. All the words in each line include the same 3-letter combination.

```
term stern later meter lighter enter painter winter counter
bail fail hail mail nail pail rail frail sail avail prevail
came fame defame frame game lame blame name same shame tame
band hand handy land sandy demand brand grand stand expands
bank blank plank rank crank drank frank shrank thank ankles
dish dismal dispels display dispose disrupt dispute distant
```

SENTENCE WRITING. You should type these sentences at top speed—especially on the second writing. They include many of the words you just practiced.

```
Hand us the dish from the counter display to dispose of it.
The same painter did enter the bank to demand blank checks.
Nail this handy rail to the plank to hold that frail stand.
She came to thank us for sending mail to that distant land.
The dispute over the name of the band may disrupt our game.
Later this winter he may sail to his dismal and sandy land.
———1———2———3———4———5———6———7———8———9———10———11———
```

RHYTHM PRACTICE. When you have mastered the drill shown at the bottom of this page, you can use it often for warm-up practice. Properly used, it will help you to develop even stroking.

Before you start typing, study the drill carefully to learn the pattern. Note that a left-hand home-row key alternates with a pair of right-hand home-row keys (;k or lj).

Your goal is an even, rhythmic tempo. You will be getting the maximum benefit from this drill only when the pause after a left-hand stroke is the same as the pause between two right-hand strokes.

Type the drill at least six times. After the first few writings, you should be able to follow the pattern without looking at your book.

```
a;ksljd;kfljg;kfljd;kslja;k  a;ksljd;kfljg;kfljd;kslja;k
```

(Message Side)   October 30, 19—*(this year)*
Dear Mr. Weston: Yes, we do plan to print the Constitution and By-Laws of the Albany Sportsmen's League. I have made a note to send you a copy. ¶ In the meantime I shall be delighted to check any details of procedure for you. Just call me any morning at 535-2647, Extension 8.   **Leo Walker, Secretary**

PROBLEM 3. *(Address Side)*   **Mr. Harvey B. Patterson   Garden Villa Apartments   Poplar Street at Ninth   Albany, New York   12203**

(Message Side)   December 3, 19—*(this year)*
Dear Mr. Patterson: The meeting on December 12 of the Albany Sportsmen's League will be Open House. Please plan to be our guest that evening. The time is 8:30 p.m. The place is the League's new building at 849 Park Avenue. We can promise a delightful program and a warm welcome.   **Leo Walker, Secretary**

TYPING ON INDEX CARDS. The first line you type on an index card will serve as a guide for filing (and finding) the card. It should, therefore, stand out from the rest of the material on the card.

Type that guide line on the second line space from the top edge. Leave a two-space margin.

Always leave one blank line space below the guide line—even though you plan to single-space the rest of your typing.

The use of all capitals for the first line is a particularly good practice when the entire card will be typed with double spacing. Note how the use of capitals in the following model helps the eye to separate the guide line from the other lines.

```
SHERMAN, HAROLD J. (DR.)

1850 Yosemite Avenue

Los Angeles, California  90008

Telephone:  727-0851
```

Model 1

Indenting the body of the card (usually three stroke spaces) will also set off the first line. Note the arrangement of Model 2 below.

```
Investments--Tuesday, March 5

   Read Chapter 16, "Endowment Insurance as
   an Investment."

   Hand in solution to Problem 1, page 385.
```

Model 2

Your Workbook contains blank forms that are the same size as standard index cards (5 inches wide by 3 inches deep). If cards are available, type the following problems on cards and use the Workbook forms for practice.

Remember to put the card holders in position before you start to type.

When you type Problems 4, 5, and 6, follow the style of Model 1. Type Problems 7 and 8 in the style of Model 2.

PROBLEM 4.   **SHERMAN, HAROLD J. (DR.)**   **1850 Yosemite Avenue   Los Angeles, California   90008**   **Telephone: 727-0851**

PROBLEM 5.   **DOYLE, OLIVE MAE (MISS)   8110 Sixth Street, N. W.   Washington, D. C.   20019   Telephone: 398-0013**

PROBLEM 6.   **BASSFORD, HELEN (MRS.)   1759 Shepherd Road   Louisville, Kentucky   40204   Telephone: 337-4210**

PROBLEM 7.   Investments—Tuesday, March 5   Read Chapter 16, "Endowment Insurance as an Investment."   Hand in solution to Problem 1, page 385.

PROBLEM 8.   Office Management—Wednesday, March 6   Have outline ready for term paper. Read Chapter 9, "Office Lighting Systems." Suggest field trip.

Line length for this lesson—60 spaces. Set margin stops. Set the line space lever at 1 until you are told to move it. Type each line on this page twice with single spacing. Double-space after each two-line group.

WARM-UP REVIEW. These lines provide a complete review of all strokes you have learned so far. Try to type with an even tempo.

Hix & Vog's #98 size holds 125 pounds; buy just 30 of them.

Did they request 4,000 of the $7 can for their 6-week sale?

TRAINING YOUR FINGERS. The four special characters in this lesson are shifts of *5, 6, 9,* and *0.* As you practice these special characters, be sure to bring your little finger back from the shift key after *each* stroke. "Shadow-type" % *space* _( ) *space* for several moments.

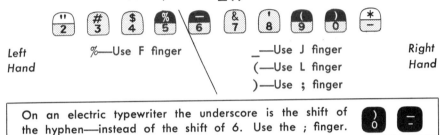

Left Hand   %—Use F finger   _—Use J finger   Right Hand

(—Use L finger

)—Use ; finger

On an electric typewriter the underscore is the shift of the hyphen—instead of the shift of 6. Use the ; finger.

KEY LOCATION PRACTICE. This drill requires special concentration.

Trust % _() Judy % _() Ohio % _() Port; % _() Portia; % _()

% _() % _() Fort % You _ Leo (Portugal) % F%T J_Y L(O (P)

Yes Joy __ Troy Toledo %% Lois Lou ((Paul Po)) _% (%) (_)

SKILL BUILDING. These sentences include every letter, every figure, and every mark or character that you have now learned.

Note: To underscore a word, first type the word; then move the carriage back to the first letter of the word, lock the shift key, and type the underscores. Remember to unlock the shift before you continue. When you must backspace more than a few spaces, you will save time by pulling the carriage back by hand.

Discounts of 20%, 10%, and 10% equal one discount of 35.2%.

This figure ($70) is 2% of the total; thus, 100% is $3,500.

The same sign (#) means both number and pounds, doesn't it?

The right net price of #73 is $100 (20%--not 15%--of $500).

Lutz & Fox may require a deposit of 20% ($40) or 25% ($50).

Their cash price ($765) is 10% below our list price ($850).

His joke (so-called) is that he can prove a dip of just 9%.

WARM-UP   They blame the giant clansman for the ambush of the airmen.

ALPHABET   He kept very large bowls of mixed frozen juices quite cold.

CONTROL   San Francisco is farther from San Antonio than Los Angeles.

TYPING THE ADDRESS ON A POSTAL CARD. For best placement of the address on a postal card, use a left margin of two inches. Type the first line slightly below the center of the card—preferably on the 12th line from the top edge. Study the following model.

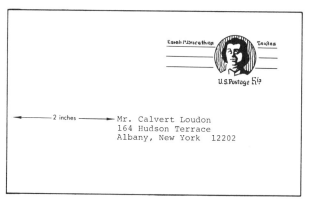

TYPING THE MESSAGE ON A POSTAL CARD. The inside address, the complimentary close, and the signature are usually omitted from a postal card. The writer's address is optional—depending upon the need for it on a particular card. When it is included, it may be typed in the upper right-hand corner above the date.

Single-space the message. Double-space between paragraphs. Study this model carefully.

```
                        1468 Stone Avenue
                        Albany, New York  12204
                        September 18, 19--

Dear Mr. Loudon:

      President Wagner has called an important
meeting of the Executive Board of the Albany
Sportsmen's League for Tuesday, September 29.

      The meeting will be held at Dr. Wagner's
home, 88 Baker Drive, at 8 p.m.  Please make
every effort to come.  We need you.

                        Leo Walker, Secretary
```

A postal card is 5½ inches wide. A line length of 4½ inches—with half-inch left and right margins—usually gives the best appearance. Try to keep the space at the top of the card and the space at the bottom of the card about equal.

The following problems are typical of cards mailed by a club secretary. Use the dates that are given. On the first card you are also to show the writer's address.

Your Workbook contains blank forms that are postal card size. If cards are available, use the forms in the Workbook for practice only.

Remember to use the card holders on your machine, as well as the paper holder. The card will often slip while you are typing unless you make sure that it is being held firmly against the platen.

PROBLEM 1. *(Address Side)*   **Mr. Calvert Loudon   164 Hudson Terrace   Albany, New York   12202**

(Message Side)   **1468 Stone Avenue   Albany, New York   12204   September 18, 19**—*(this year)*

Dear **Mr. Loudon:**   President **Wagner has called an important meeting of the Executive Board of the Albany Sportsmen's League for Tuesday, September 29. ¶ The meeting will be held at Dr. Wagner's home, 88 Baker Drive, at 8 p.m. Please make every effort to come. We need you.   Leo Walker, Secretary**

PROBLEM 2. *(Address Side)*   **Mr. Larry C. Weston   1305 Lake Avenue   Albany, New York   12204**

WORD DRILL. All the words in each line contain the same 3-letter combination. Train yourself to type by letter groups—not letter by letter.

```
fire hire mire admire spire aspire desire tires retire wire
own owns owner down gown clown brown crown drown frown town
bound found ground pound compound round sound bounce ounces
out outer outlay outmost scout about clout spout rout stout
taught caught eight height weight fight flight ought fought
mint mined mineral mingle minor minus minutes remind famine
```

SENTENCE WRITING. Most of the words in these sentences are words that you have just practiced. Type these sentences smoothly—at your top speed.

```
The owner of this ground found out about its mineral worth.
Remind the clown to bounce the round tires down the stairs.
The weight of one pound minus eight ounces is eight ounces.
The brown spire caught fire during the height of the fight.
Do not hire that scout if his own town does not admire him.
The stout clown may drown if he goes beyond the outer wire.
```
———1———2———3———4———5———6———7———8———9———10———11———

PARAGRAPH PREVIEW. Some of these words often cause hesitation. Type them with a smooth, even tempo. Try to speed up on the second writing.

```
as expert be are need skill suffer smoothly striking unless
devote develop acquire quality recognize practice technique
```

PARAGRAPH TYPING. *Move the line space lever to 2. Set a stop for a 5-space indention.* Type this paragraph line for line. It contains the entire alphabet.

Words

```
    The quality of your work is going to suffer unless you      11
recognize the need to develop expert skill in making use of    23
the shift key and unless you acquire skill in making shifts    35
without losing much time.  If you are not striking capitals    47
so easily and so smoothly as the job should be done, devote    59
more thought and time to the practice of this technique.       70
```
———1———2———3———4———5———6———7———8———9———10———11———

PROBLEMS IN ENVELOPE ADDRESSING. The following twenty addresses are the envelope addresses for the letters that you have typed in this course. You are to type all of them in the block style with open punctuation.

Unless your instructor tells you otherwise, type the first ten addresses on No. 6¾ envelopes and type the remaining ten addresses on No. 10 envelopes.

Note: Your Workbook contains two sheets that explain how to fold a letter for insertion in a No. 6¾ or a No. 10 envelope. Practice the correct folding of a letter by following the directions on these sheets.

1. Mr. Gerald D. Morrison   930 West Keller Street   Buffalo, NY   14221

2. Wallace & Anderson, Inc.   2638 Pioneer Boulevard   Oakland, CA   94604

3. H. H. Darlington and Sons, Inc.   Broad Street at Third Avenue   Chattanooga, TN   37401

4. Mr. Leonard J. Mifflin   2963 North Fifth Street   Madison, WI   53704

5. Dr. Samuel R. Westbury   53 East Valley Road   Lawrenceburg, KY   40342

6. Mr. Vance Bryson, Sports Editor   Louisville Tribune-Sentinel   Kentucky News Building   Louisville, KY   40203

7. Mr. Henry V. Kane, President   Westco Manufacturing Company   450 West Seventh Avenue   Jeffersonville, IN   47130

8. Miss Nancy D. Parker   847 Hillcrest Street   Decatur, IL   62521

9. Mr. Keith J. Davis, Manager   Sloan Upholstery Company   23 South Prescott Street   Oklahoma City, OK   73102

10. Mrs. Roscoe D. Hall, Jr.   1806 West 35th Street   Los Angeles, CA   90009

11. Mr. Floyd B. Greerson   305 West Boulder Avenue   Kent Gardens   Los Angeles, CA   90007

12. Roney Manufacturing Company   Attention of Mr. H. R. Nolan   2847 North Erie Boulevard   Cleveland, OH   44118

13. Mr. Paul G. Wells, Sales Manager   Cuttle Implement Company, Inc.   Foster Avenue and 95th Street   Chicago, IL   60614

14. Mr. C. G. Hood, Secretary   New England Hobby League   675 West Vermont Avenue   Portland, ME   04102

15. Miss Phyllis J. Ware, President   Fashion Associates, Inc.   1739 Park Avenue   New York, NY   10018

16. Department N-8   Warren & Carvelle, Inc.   9120 South Morgan Street   St. Louis, MO   63109

17. Miss Helen B. Richards   Director of Advertising   The A. H. Gault Company   23rd and Maple Streets   Hartford, CT   06102

18. Mr. Henry V. Brent, President   Brent Construction Company   1394 North 15th Street   San Antonio, TX   78202

19. Mr. N. S. Watkins, Secretary   Easterwood Advertising Agency   Elm and McDonnell Streets   Philadelphia, PA   19120

20. Midland Paper Corporation   Attention of Credit Manager   2500 North Mill Street   Detroit, MI   48218

LESSON 15

Timed Typing

Line length for this page—70 spaces. Set margin stops. Set the line space lever at 2. Set a stop for a 5-space paragraph indention. Type the paragraphs numbered 1 and 2 as a continuous article with double spacing. Omit the numbers. Listen for the bell!

REINSERTING A TYPED SHEET. After you have removed a typed sheet from your machine, you may sometimes have to reinsert it to make a change or an addition.

The following paragraphs contain helpful hints on how to do that work well. Before you type the paragraphs as a timed writing, read through them for the information they give.

Words

1 Now and then you will have to reinsert a sheet in your machine to 13
add a letter or to correct some other kind of error; you will have no 27
trouble in doing so if you observe a few basic principles and if you 41
make full use of the devices placed on your machine to assist you in 55
such work. Sometimes the sheet will fall automatically into its 68
correct position when you feed it back into the machine; far more 81
often, however, some adjustment is going to be needed before you 94
can safely start to type. After the paper has been fed into your 107
machine, check first of all to make sure that the line of writing is 121
straight; if it slants a little, use the paper release to free the paper 136
while you adjust the sheet carefully with both hands. When you 148
are sure that you have the line perfectly straight, use the variable line 163
spacer to get the line in correct relationship to the line scale; turn the 178
platen up or down slowly until the typed letters just clear the line 192
scale. 193

↓

2 Your next check for correct position involves making certain that 13   206
the typed letters are centered perfectly over the markers on the line 27   221
scale. Make that check by examining the position of a period or of 41   234
a letter that has a definite mid-point; the mid-point should, of course, 55   248
be in a direct line with the marker. In case some adjustment must 69   262
be made, again use the paper release and slide the paper very slightly 83   276
to the right or to the left until you see that it is in perfect position. 98   291
Before you do any typing, make a final check by striking very lightly 112   305
over a typed letter. If the sheet is back in its original position, the 127   320
stroke you make will not be visible; if the sheet still needs adjust- 140   333
ment, you will see your stroke as a faint shadow beside the letter. 154   347
The safest way to make this check is to put the ribbon indicator on 168   361
stencil position; the only impression that the key can then make is a 182   375
very faint mark caused by the ink still clinging to it. 193   386

Addressing Envelopes

WARM-UP   They did risk the usual profit when they bid for the docks.

ALPHABET   Viola is making chintz pads for their square jewelry boxes.

CONTROL   Alan Lake may visit Spain and Italy when he goes to Europe.

ENVELOPE SIZES. The two most widely used envelope sizes are called the "No. 6¾," which measures 6½ inches by 3⅝ inches, and the larger "No. 10," which measures 9½ by 4⅛ inches.

Study the rules given below for addressing envelopes of both sizes.

PROPER POSITION. Leave a left margin of 2½ inches on the small (No. 6¾) envelope. Start to type on the 13th line space from the top edge.

On the larger envelope (the No. 10), leave a left margin of 4 inches and start typing on the 15th line space from the top edge.

Addressing Envelopes

Clark BROTHERS, INC.

Mr. Keith J. Davis, Manager
Sloan Upholstery Company
23 South Prescott Street
Oklahoma City, Oklahoma 73102

To aid automatic mail-sorting equipment, block and single-space all addresses.

MELVIN TRASK & SONS

Roney Manufacturing Company
Attention of Mr. H. R. Nolan
2847 North Erie Boulevard
Cleveland, Ohio 44118

When there is an attention line, type it on the second line of the envelope address.

Monroe LABEL COMPANY
1600 EAST 80TH STREET
NEW YORK, NEW YORK 10005

Midland Paper Corporation
2500 North Mill Street
Detroit, MI 48218

Type the city, the state name or abbreviation, and the ZIP Code on the last line.

WORD DRILL. These lines stress certain high-frequency 3-letter combinations. All words in a line contain the same combination.

```
list listen fist vocalist wrist resist insist consist twist
cute acute lute dilute mute minute compute computer dispute
cure procure obscure endure lure pure impure mature gesture
ample amplify example camp damp lamp clamp ramp cramp stamp
dine fine define shine line mine nine pine spine twine vine
ore core score shore more ignore snore sore tore store wore
```

SENTENCE WRITING. The words you just practiced are used in these sentences. Watch for the 3-letter combinations.

```
Go nine miles to the mine to procure more ore for the camp.
Ignore the obscure vocalist for one minute to listen to us.
Define the fine line that divides the pure from the impure.
An example of mine is to twist fine twine to form the line.
Ignore the dispute and compute her score with the computer.
An acute sore may resist cure if they dilute pure medicine.
———1———2———3———4———5———6———7———8———9———10———11———
```

PARAGRAPH PREVIEW. Many of these words have double letters. Try to type them with a smooth, even tempo—without jerkiness.

```
on ribbon speed mess carefully will actually ready threaded
see replace typewriter amazed quickly expertly least rather
```

PARAGRAPH TYPING. *Move the line space lever to 2. Set a stop for a 5-space indention.* This paragraph contains the whole alphabet. Type it line for line.

	Words
When the time comes to replace the worn ribbon on your	11
typewriter with a new one, you have to be ready to make the	23
change with the least mess and the most speed. The job can	35
be rather easy if you study carefully the way the ribbon is	47
threaded on the machine; you will actually be amazed to see	59
how quickly and expertly this important job can be done.	70

```
———1———2———3———4———5———6———7———8———9———10———11———
```

PROBLEM 3. Type this letter in the full-block style with open punctuation. Use Form 7-3. Note the enclosure notation.

(79 words in body)

Mr. N. S. Watkins, Secretary   Easterwood Advertising Agency   Elm and McDonnell Streets   Philadelphia, PA 19120
Dear Mr. Watkins   Thank you for your order for 25 rolls of address labels and for the check that you enclosed. ¶ You have included in the amount of your check the extra charge for color. Will any one of the four regular colors—pink, green, blue, or yellow—be all right? ¶ Please fill in and mail the enclosed card to let us know the color or assortment of colors you prefer. Shipment will be made the same day we hear from you.   Sincerely yours
MONROE LABEL COMPANY   Order Department   CWR: Enclosure

PROBLEM 4. Type this letter in the full-block style with open punctuation. Use Form 7-4. Note that the letter has an attention line and an enclosure notation. *The body of the letter contains all the figures on the keyboard.*

(63 words in body)

Midland Paper Corporation   2500 North Mill Street   Detroit, MI 48218   Attention of Credit Manager   Gentlemen   Our check for $3,759.40 is enclosed with this letter. You will note on the voucher portion of the check that we have deducted the time discount of 2%, as authorized in your letter of March 16. ¶ According to our own records, the enclosed check reduces the balance on our account to $8,270.31. Please notify us promptly in case your records do not agree.   Very truly yours
MONROE LABEL COMPANY   Accounting Department   NIO: Enclosure

---

Abbreviations of State Names

(Also District of Columbia, Guam, Puerto Rico, and Virgin Islands)

Alabama	AL	Kentucky	KY	Ohio	OH
Alaska	AK	Louisiana	LA	Oklahoma	OK
Arizona	AZ	Maine	ME	Oregon	OR
Arkansas	AR	Maryland	MD	Pennsylvania	PA
California	CA	Massachusetts	MA	Puerto Rico	PR
Colorado	CO	Michigan	MI	Rhode Island	RI
Connecticut	CT	Minnesota	MN	South Carolina	SC
Delaware	DE	Mississippi	MS	South Dakota	SD
District of Columbia	DC	Missouri	MO	Tennessee	TN
Florida	FL	Montana	MT	Texas	TX
Georgia	GA	Nebraska	NE	Utah	UT
Guam	GU	Nevada	NV	Vermont	VT
Hawaii	HI	New Hampshire	NH	Virginia	VA
Idaho	ID	New Jersey	NJ	Virgin Islands	VI
Illinois	IL	New Mexico	NM	Washington	WA
Indiana	IN	New York	NY	West Virginia	WV
Iowa	IA	North Carolina	NC	Wisconsin	WI
Kansas	KS	North Dakota	ND	Wyoming	WY

LESSON 16
" * ½ ¢

Line length for this lesson—60 spaces. Set margin stops. Set the line space lever at 1. Type each line on this page twice with single spacing. Double-space after each two-line group.

WARM-UP REVIEW. These lines will help you to check your mastery of the keyboard and of the shift keys. They include every stroke you have learned.

Invoice #9364 ($7,820) is marked net; write a check for it.
Didn't Galtz & Company pack just 15% of their 72-qt. boxes?

TRAINING YOUR FINGERS. Two characters in this lesson—½ and ¢— are new reaches. Locate them on the keyboard. The quotation marks (") and the asterisk (*) are shifts of keys on the top row.

After you feel that you know the locations of all four keys, "shadow-type" " *space* *½¢ *space* for several moments.

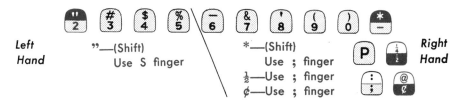

Left Hand

"—(Shift)
Use S finger

*—(Shift)
Use ; finger
½—Use ; finger
¢—Use ; finger

Right Hand

On an electric typewriter the ¢ is the shift of 6 (J finger), and the * is the shift of 8 (K finger). The " is the shift of the apostrophe (; finger).

KEY LOCATION PRACTICE. These lines call for your close attention. Remember that you shift for " and for *—not for ½ or ¢. Watch your spacing!

Shaw " *½¢ Paris " *½¢ prop; " *½¢ goal; " *½¢ prowl; " *½¢
" *½¢ " *½¢ Swiss " Peru; * top; ½ repel; ¢ "½" ¢½¢ "*" ½"¢
West Swift "" Persia; Porto; ** hop; shop; ½½ owl; howl; ¢¢

SKILL BUILDING. These sentences make extensive use of the new keys. They also include all the other strokes you have now learned.

The price rose from 8½¢ to 12½¢ last month; now it is 15½¢.
Dix & Jove quoted 39½¢--7½¢ less than your "special" price.
He "thinks" the only way to mark notes is with *'s and #'s.
"The stock," he said, "may go to 106½; today's bid is 94½."
Since ½ is ½% of 100, ½% of $1.00 (100¢) is one half of 1¢.
The asterisk (*) marks an item cut from 98¢ a dozen to 50¢.
He asked, "Do they expect us to come down 2½¢ or 3½¢ more?"

WARM-UP   The oak shelf is the right shape and height for their work.

ALPHABET   Paula might give one box of quartz rocks to the wily judge.

CONTROL   The commander of troops will soon see all skilled officers.

FULL-BLOCK LETTER STYLE. The body of the letter in Problem 1 explains the full-block letter style. Study it carefully. As you do so, refer to the illustration at the right.

This letter also illustrates the use of open punctuation. Full-block letters may be typed with either mixed or open punctuation.

PROBLEM 1. Type this letter in the full-block style with open punctuation. Use Form 7-1. The illustration on this page shows how the letter looks when it is typed on a pica-type machine.

The body of the letter contains all the letters of the alphabet.

(136 words in body)

Miss Helen B. Richards   Director of Advertising   The A. H. Gault Company   23rd and Maple Streets   Hartford, Connecticut   06102 Dear Miss Richards   The style in which this letter is typed is called the full-block letter style. All parts of the letter, including the date and the lines at the end of the letter, start at the left margin. ¶ Because there is no need to set tabulator stops, the use of the full-block style saves time. This style is often authorized, therefore, in offices where top speed is rated above appearance. It is not yet, however, used nearly so extensively as either the block or the semiblock style. ¶ When open punctuation is chosen, as it was for this letter, there is no colon after the salutation—just as there is no comma after the complimentary close. ¶ Open punctuation is most frequently seen with the full-block letter style. It may also be used with the block or the semiblock style. Sincerely yours   PALMER & LESTER   Production Manager   RWB:

PROBLEM 2. Type this letter in the full-block style with open punctuation. Use Form 7-2. *The body of the letter contains all the letters of the alphabet.* *(52 words in body)*

Mr. Henry V. Brent, President   Brent Construction Company   1394 North 15th Street San Antonio, TX   78202   Dear Mr. Brent The United States Postal Service authorizes the use of two-letter, all-capital abbreviations for states, the District of Columbia, and major possessions. Make an extra effort to learn them. ¶ Do not type a period following the abbreviation. You are requested to leave two spaces between the abbreviation and the ZIP Code. Sincerely yours   MONROE LABEL COMPANY   Supervisor   ARA:

Speed Building

Type each line of Word Drill and Sentence Writing twice with single spacing. Double-space after each two-line group.

WORD DRILL. All the 3-letter high-frequency combinations in this group of words contain the letter *a*. Each line has a different combination.

```
cash dash gash lash clash flash slash smash rash crash wash

deal dealer heal realm seal squeal veal zeal conceal repeal

last blast past paste least plastic toast roast coast boast

entrance rancor enhance anchor ancient dance glance finance

angle angry anger hang clang rang range strange sprang sang

artful article heart mart part particle apart depart impart
```

SENTENCE WRITING. These speed-building sentences include a large number of the words you have just practiced. Push for speed!

```
The rash dealer did cash the last bond to finance the deal.

Artful use of plastic tape to seal the gash may conceal it.

The last part of this angry article shows the least rancor.

They sprang into the strange dance from some ancient realm.

Dash to the last entrance and urge the angry mob to depart.

The strange blast did smash an ancient city near the coast.
```
——1——2——3——4——5——6——7——8——9——10——11——

RHYTHM PRACTICE. The home-row drill shown at the bottom of this page is especially good for practice because it will help you to improve the evenness of your stroking. When you have learned the drill pattern, use it often for warm-up practice.

This drill follows the same general plan of the drill you learned in Lesson 13, but the hands are used in reverse order. Note that—in this case—a right-hand stroke on the home row alternates with two left-hand strokes on the home row (ad or sf).

It will help you to "shadow-type" the drill a couple of times to familiarize yourself with the pattern. After you start typing the drill, the fingering will soon become automatic.

Type this drill at least six times. Remember that your goal is even stroking.

```
;adlsfkadjsfhadjsfkadlsf;ad   ;adlsfkadjsfhadjsfkadlsf;ad
```

```
                              2947 Pine Street
                              Dayton, Ohio  45404
                              April 29, 19--



Mr. C. G. Hood, Secretary
New England Hobby League
675 West Vermont Avenue
Portland, Maine  04102

Dear Mr. Hood:

     When you type a business letter on plain paper,
include your complete address, along with the date,
at the top of the letter.  For personal-business
letters, it is usually best to start these lines at
the center of the sheet, as shown here.

     Start your own address on the tenth line from
the top if the body of your letter is fairly long--
200 words or more.  Drop to the eleventh or twelfth
line for shorter letters.

     Vary the space between the date and the start
of the inside address with the length of the letter.
There should be at least two blank line spaces below
the date.  The usual number is four.

     To get good letter placement on plain paper,
start the inside address a line or two higher than
its starting point on a letterhead.  The bottom mar-
gin of your letter should be slightly wider than
the top margin.

                              Sincerely yours,



                              Marjorie N. Wilkinson
                              (Mrs. John B. Wilkinson)
```

Model Letter 4—Personal-Business Letter

Semiblock Style—Mixed Punctuation

Line length: 5 inches   Words in body: 152

Heading starts: Line 11   Inside address starts: Line 18

LESSON 17

Timed Typing

Line length for this page—70 spaces. Set margin stops. Set the line space lever at 2. Set a stop for a 5-space paragraph indention. Type the paragraphs numbered 1 and 2 as a continuous article. Omit the numbers. Listen for the bell!

CHANGING A RIBBON. The practical hints given in the two paragraphs on this page will help you to change your typewriter ribbon quickly and easily. Before you type the paragraphs, read them for the information they contain.

Words

1 When the time comes to remove a worn ribbon from your machine — 12
and to replace it with a new one, you want to be ready to make the — 26
change with the smallest amount of mess and the greatest possible — 39
speed. The job is really quite simple when you observe a few basic — 53
principles of procedure; you will actually be astonished to see how — 66
quickly the task can be done. Before you try to take out the old — 79
ribbon, move the carriage to the center of your machine and depress — 93
the shift lock; then put the ribbon indicator on red position and de- — 107
press two central keys until they lock together. If you watch your — 120
machine as you make these operations, you will notice that they have — 134
the effect of bringing the ribbon out into the open where you can — 147
easily work with it.   The final stage in preparing to change ribbons is — 162
to make a careful study of the way the ribbon is threaded on the — 175
machine; when you have a clear-cut picture of the ribbon path, you — 188
are ready to remove the worn ribbon. — 195

2 Roll the worn ribbon entirely on one spool, take a final look at the — 14 — 209
ribbon path, and then disengage the ribbon from the ribbon guide — 27 — 222
and detach it from the empty spool. After you lift out the spool of — 41 — 236
worn ribbon, unroll several inches of the new ribbon and hook the — 54 — 249
end to the empty spool; then drop both spools into position on your — 67 — 262
typewriter. The job of threading the new ribbon through the guide — 81 — 276
is best done last--after you have had a chance to make sure that both — 95 — 290
spools are firmly seated and that the ribbon is straight. When you — 108 — 303
have the new ribbon in place, remember that two keys have been — 121 — 316
locked together while you have been changing ribbons. Be sure to — 134 — 329
release those keys and to tap one of the shift keys to release the shift — 149 — 344
lock. The last step before you start to type on the new ribbon, of — 162 — 357
course, is to move the ribbon indicator from red position to blue — 176 — 371
position; your machine is then ready once again for operation in the — 189 — 384
usual way. — 191 — 386

WARM-UP   He got an authentic map of the big city to aid the visitor.

ALPHABET   Kathy may give two nice prizes for the mixed jonquil bulbs.

CONTROL   Three committees will greet all school applicants tomorrow.

PROBLEM 1. Study Model Letter 4 on the next page. The body of the letter contains suggestions for typing your personal-business letters.

Type Model Letter 4.

PROBLEM 2. Read through the following letter. It contains additional information about the typing of personal-business letters.

Type this letter in the semiblock style. *The body of the letter contains all the letters of the alphabet.*

(194 words in body)

Crestview Apartments   811 Madison Street York, Pennsylvania 17402   *(Today's date)* Miss Phyllis J. Ware, President   Fashion Associates, Inc.   1739 Park Avenue   New York, New York 10018   Dear Miss Ware: Your address should appear on the envelope in which you mail a business letter. Remember, though, that envelopes are discarded in many offices before letters are routed to various executives or departments. Be sure that the address you type at the top of your letter is complete in every detail. ¶ Your typed name is equally important. The signature that is perfectly clear to you and to your friends will likely be just a puzzle to a stranger. ¶ It is understood in business that a person who uses initials or whose first name is not obviously feminine is to be addressed as Mr. in reply. A man does not, therefore, type Mr. with his name or write the title in his signature. ¶ In the same way an unmarried woman omits Miss from her typed name. If she uses initials or if her name might be thought of as being masculine, however, she should write the title—in parentheses—before her signature. ¶ When,

on the other hand, a woman is married, the signature section of her letter should indicate that fact. Note again how the names are typed at the end of Model Letter 4. Sincerely yours, Mary W. Corrigan

PROBLEM 3. Use your own home address and your own name on the following letter.

Note the abbreviation *c.o.d.* in the body of the letter. When you type abbreviations that consist of single small letters, type the small letters "solid," thus:

c.o.d.   a.m.

f.o.b.   p.m.

Type the letter in the semiblock style. *The body of the letter contains all the letters of the alphabet.*

(121 words in body)

Department N-8   Warren & Carvelle, Inc. 9120 South Morgan Street   St. Louis, Missouri 63109   Gentlemen: About ten days ago I sent you my order on your special order form for one desk lamp—Stock No. 52. I enclosed my check for the quoted price of $7.95. According to your offer, the lamp was then to come to me postpaid. ¶ Today the postman brought me a c.o.d. package from you and asked me to pay him $8. Because I realized that there had been a mistake, I rejected the package. ¶ My bank reports that the check I sent you has come back all right with your endorsement. ¶ Please arrange to have my lamp delivered to me without extra cost. The postman tells me that the package he had with him today can be identified as No. 403199. Sincerely yours,

Speed Building

Set stops for a 60-space line. Set the line space lever at 1. Except for the paragraph, type each line twice. Double-space after each two-line group.

WORD DRILL. The 3-letter high-frequency combinations in these lines will help you to add to your speed. All the words in each line contain the same combination.

```
inch pinch clinch incline include incur zinc since convince
sing sting ring bring wring spring string cling fling sling
bite white kite polite ignite unite spite write site invite
dive five give live revive drive river derive thrive strive
elect reflect neglect object project inspect expect protect
tight light delight slight mighty tonight night right sight
```

SENTENCE WRITING. These fast sentences make extensive use of the words you just practiced. Try to push up your speed.

```
Sight of the mighty river should give the five men delight.
He may convince her that any white kite does reflect light.
Invite her to drive here tonight and bring the zinc object.
Include white string to hold this ring to the right spring.
Five polite boys may unite to sing tonight for our delight.
Strive to elect men who would unite to revive this project.
```
———1———2———3———4———5———6———7———8———9———10———11———

PARAGRAPH PREVIEW. Concentrate on the fingering of these words. This practice will help you type the paragraph more smoothly.

```
one are get eraser erase keep sheet erasure will well amaze
card carbons avoid smearing placing typing obtained results
```

PARAGRAPH TYPING. *Move the line space lever to 2. Set a stop for a 5-space indention.* This paragraph contains the entire alphabet. Type it line for line.

	Words
If you are typing one or more carbons and must make an	11
erasure, you can keep the copies from smearing by placing a	23
card just in back of the sheet on which you erase. Use any	35
soft eraser for carbon copies, making sure to keep it clean	47
to avoid smearing the work. Just an ordinary pencil eraser	59
works quite well; expert results obtained will amaze you.	70

———1———2———3———4———5———6———7———8———9———10———11———

WARM-UP   It is right for them to pay us for the six bushels of corn.

ALPHABET   Their jeweler bought me six topaz rings for quick delivery.

CONTROL   Tillie will soon discuss that matter with three good cooks.

ATTENTION LINE. Type an attention line two line spaces below the inside address and two line spaces above the salutation. Start at the left margin in either a semiblock or a block letter.

The wording and arrangement of the attention line depend upon office practice. The style illustrated here is widely used.

To get the best placement for a letter with an attention line, start the letter one line above the usual starting point.

```
Roney Manufacturing Company
2847 North Erie Boulevard
Cleveland, Ohio  44118

Attention of Mr. H. R. Nolan

Gentlemen:

Please refer to our Purchase Order 9132 and to your
Invoice 6483 for 93½ dozen No. 5840-B and 15¼ dozen
```

PROBLEM 1. This letter has an attention line. Type the letter in the block style. Use Form 5-1. *The body of the letter contains all the letters, figures, characters, and punctuation marks on the keyboard.*

(110 words in body)

Roney Manufacturing Company   2847 North Erie Boulevard   Cleveland, Ohio   44118 Attention of Mr. H. R. Nolan   Gentlemen: Please refer to our Purchase Order 9132 and to your Invoice 6483 for 93½ dozen No. 5840-B and 15¼ dozen No. 2736-Q. ¶ When delivery was made by Dow & Sax Freight Company (B/L 2849), we had to pay freight charges of $8.82 (900# @ 98¢ C). ¶ The note at the bottom of page 12 of your catalog reads as follows: "Note: On items marked with an asterisk (*), we pay 50% of the freight charges." ¶ Both items on this order are so marked in your catalog; your Invoice 6483, however, doesn't show any credit to apply against the freight charges we paid. Shall we just deduct

$4.41 when we write our check for the invoice? Very truly yours,   **MELVIN TRASK & SONS**   Frank G. Cassidy

SUBJECT LINE. A subject line is typed two line spaces below the salutation and two line spaces above the first paragraph. It may be centered horizontally. Most typists prefer, however, to start the subject line at the same point at which the paragraphs start.

Type a colon after the word *Subject*. Leave two spaces after the colon.

Provide for the subject line by raising the starting point of the letter one line.

```
Mr. Paul G. Wells, Sales Manager
Cuttle Implement Company, Inc.
Foster Avenue and 95th Street
Chicago, Illinois  60614

Dear Mr. Wells:

Subject:  Model 9-R Garden Tractor

When you visited us last month, you told
us that this model has been redesigned.
```

PROBLEM 2. Type this letter in the block style. Use Form 5-2. The letter has a subject line.

(60 words in body)

Mr. Paul G. Wells, Sales Manager   Cuttle Implement Company, Inc.   Foster Avenue and 95th Street   Chicago, Illinois   60614 Dear Mr. Wells: Subject: Model 9-R Garden Tractor   When you visited us last month, you told us that this model has been redesigned. We understood that the new tractor would probably be ready for the market within a few weeks. Can you now give us a definite date? ¶ Our stock is getting low. If we can do so, we want to wait for the new tractor before re-ordering.   Cordially yours,   **MELVIN TRASK & SONS**   Purchasing Agent   **MKL:**

LESSON 18
¼ @ : /

Line length for this lesson—60 spaces. Set margin stops. Set the line space lever at 1 until you are told to move it. Type each line on this page twice with single spacing. Double-space after each two-line group.

WARM-UP REVIEW. These lines include every stroke you have learned. You will be wise to reduce your speed deliberately and to concentrate on absolute accuracy.

"Why," asked Joe McQuade, "is the 46½-lb. size $1.75 more?"
Van & Gup's #95 box is up 30%; an asterisk (*) follows 28¢.

TRAINING YOUR FINGERS. The four special characters in this lesson are made with reaches you have already learned. They are typed with the semicolon finger.

When you have located the keys, look away from the keyboard and "shadow-type" ¼@:/ *space* for several moments. Be sure to bring your left little finger back from the shift key after each shifted stroke.

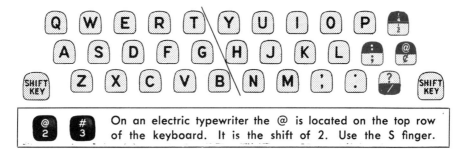

On an electric typewriter the @ is located on the top row of the keyboard. It is the shift of 2. Use the S finger.

KEY LOCATION PRACTICE. Pay close attention to your spacing as you type these lines. You may find it helpful to say each character to yourself as you type.

;½¢; Lake; ¼@:/ Park; ¼@:/ Kent; ¼@:/ Ohio; ¼@:/ July; ¼@:/
l/c; a/c; and/or; n/f; his/her; 11:1; Jack:; 1:11; to wit:;
½ and ¼; ¼¢; 1¼¢; ¼ of 1½¢; @ 1¢; @ 1½¢; @ ½¢; @ 1¼¢; @ ¼¢;

SKILL BUILDING. Every letter, punctuation mark, figure, and special character on the keyboard is included in this group of sentences.

A 2:40 bus gets here at 6:20, and the 3:50 arrives at 8:05.
She replied: "The new low price is 48 2/5¢--down 33 1/3%."
Jux & Quaker stock came down from 93¼ to 72¼ by 3:15 today.
They billed us for 48 @ $1.38 a dozen and for 5 @ 3¼¢ each.
What is the sum of 9 @ 5 1/6¢, 82 @ 4 1/3¢, and 7 @ 3 5/6¢?
Style #84 is 5½' by 7¼'; the next size (#85) is 6¼' by 8¼'.
When there is an asterisk (*), add 4¼%; otherwise, add 2¼%.

Clark BROTHERS, INC.

Southern California's foremost decorators of the home

Third Street at Del Rio — Los Angeles, California 90005

June 23, 19--

Miss Nancy D. Parker
847 Hillcrest Street
Decatur, Illinois 62521

Dear Miss Parker:

When a letter is typed in the block style,
the paragraphs start at the left margin.
In all other respects the block style is
identical with the semiblock style.

You may start the date at the center or
type it to end at the right margin. Use
the style adopted by the office in which
you work.

The way in which identifying initials are
typed on a letter depends upon personal
preference rather than upon letter style.
On this letter, for example, the initials
of the typist are shown in small letters.
Those of the dictator are omitted.

                        Sincerely yours,

                        CLARK BROTHERS, INC.

                        Vernon W. Clark

xxx

Model Letter 3—Block Style Business Letter

Mixed Punctuation

Line length: 4 inches   Words in body: 98

Date: Line 14   Inside address starts: Line 23

Note: To type the date in the position used for this letter, first
move the carriage to the right margin. Then backspace once for each
character and space in the date and begin to type.

WORD DRILL. The same 3-letter high-frequency combination appears in all the words in any one line. Type each combination as a letter group!

bound abound found pound compound round around ground sound

coke broke spoke woke awoke revoke choke stoke smoke stroke

wise unwise likewise otherwise rise arise surprise disguise

harbor hard harden hardly hardship harm harmful harsh sharp

speak special specialty specific specimen speck spend spent

stack stadium stale stalk stake static station stain stairs

SENTENCE WRITING. The words you just practiced are extensively used in these sentences. Type the sentences at your best rate.

They can hardly pound one sharp stake into the hard ground.

Harmful coke smoke may otherwise rise from the round stack.

It is hardly wise to station special men around the harbor.

One hard stroke broke the stalk of the specimen they found.

It is likewise unwise to speak about any specific hardship.

She awoke with surprise to the harsh sound of sharp static.

————1————2————3————4————5————6————7————8————9———10———11————

PARAGRAPH PREVIEW. All the words in these two lines appear in the following paragraph. Practice on them will improve your paragraph typing rate.

no not part attention keep excellent accumulated will bills

every typewriter service wizard you few designed mechanical

PARAGRAPH TYPING. *Move the line space lever to 2. Set a tab stop for a 5-space indention.* Type this paragraph line for line with double spacing.

	Words
Although the typewriter is designed and made to take a	11
lot of abuse, it does require a certain amount of attention	23
if it is to keep on giving excellent service with few or no	35
repair bills. You do not have to be a mechanical wizard to	47
do your part; just spending a minute every morning brushing	59
out any accumulated grit or dust will pay big dividends.	70

————1————2————3————4————5————6————7————8————9———10———11————

WARM-UP   They lent me their big bicycle to rush to town for the key.

ALPHABET   The jury examined bronze plaques taken from covered wagons.

CONTROL   Ellen peeled fifteen green apples to make her apple butter.

PROBLEM 1. Make a careful study of Model Letter 3 on the next page. The body of the letter explains the difference between the block style and the semiblock style.

Type Model Letter 3 on Form 4-1.

PROBLEM 2. Type the following letter in the block style. Use Form 4-2.

The body of the letter contains all the letters of the alphabet.

(84 words in body)

Mr. Keith J. Davis, Manager   Sloan Upholstery Company   23 South Prescott Street Oklahoma City, Oklahoma 73102   Dear Mr. Davis: Many people feel that the initials of the dictator are never required when his name is typed in full at the end of the letter. You will often see letters, therefore, on which just the initials of the typist are shown. ¶ Sometimes the omission of the dictator's initials is also authorized when the name of the dictator is printed at the top of the letterhead. If the reader cannot be sure what the signature is, he can check the name by examining the letterhead.   Sincerely yours,   CLARK BROTHERS, INC.   M. W. McAllister

PROBLEM 3. This letter has an enclosure notation. Type the letter in the block style. Use Form 4-3.

(65 words in body)

Mrs. Roscoe D. Hall, Jr.   1806 West 35th Street   Los Angeles, California 90009 Dear Mrs. Hall: Perhaps your check for $94.72 is already in the mail. If it is, please disregard this friendly reminder that your latest bill is now overdue. You have always paid your other bills so promptly that I know you just overlooked the due date. ¶ A duplicate of the bill is enclosed. I am also enclosing a stamped envelope that you may use to mail your check.   Sincerely yours,   CLARK BROTHERS, INC.   Martin N. Thomas Enclosures 2

PROBLEM 4. The following letter also has an enclosure notation. Type the letter in the block style. Use Form 4-4.

(173 words in body)

Mr. Floyd B. Greerson   305 West Boulder Avenue   Kent Gardens   Los Angeles, California 90007 Dear Mr. Greerson: Congratulations to you and to Mrs. Greerson on the purchase of your lovely new home in Kent Gardens. As many of your new neighbors are loyal customers of Clark Brothers, I have made frequent visits in your community. I know that you are going to like it enormously. Kent Gardens has always been known for its friendly folks, as well as for the charm of its homes. ¶ I want to extend to you the same warm welcome here at Clark Brothers that I am sure you are receiving from your new neighbors. Please come in to see us often. When you have decorating plans or decorating problems, I hope you will remember that the advice of our experts is always yours for the asking. ¶ I am especially happy to enclose with this letter an application form for your use in opening a charge account. Please fill in the form and mail it to me, so that I may send you your personal credit card at once. Credit at Clark Brothers costs you nothing.   Cordially yours,   CLARK BROTHERS, INC. Frank Thomas Clark   Enclosure

LESSON 19

Timed Typing

Line length for this page—70 spaces. Set margin stops. Set the line space lever at 2 for double spacing. Set a stop for a 5-space indention. Type the paragraphs numbered 1 and 2 as a continuous article. Omit the numbers. Listen for the bell!

CARBON COPIES. Whenever you apply your typing skill to typical typing jobs, you will usually want to make one or more carbon copies. Now is the time to learn proper techniques.

The two paragraphs below discuss the making of carbon copies and give suggestions about erasing on them. Before you type the paragraphs, read them carefully for the information they contain.

Words

1 It is a good idea to get into the habit of assembling papers for a | 13
carbon pack by building up the pack from the back. If you are | 26
making only one carbon copy, put down the copy sheet first on your | 39
desk, lay the carbon paper on it with the carbon side down, and then | 53
add the original sheet or letterhead face up on top of the pack. This | 67
habit will become particularly valuable to you when you have to | 80
make several carbon copies because it will help you to make sure | 93
that you have precisely the correct number of copy sheets, the right | 107
amount of carbon paper, and that the carbon paper faces in the right | 121
direction. After you have assembled the pack, take it in both hands | 135
and tap it on your desk until all the edges are even; then insert the | 149
pack exactly as you would a single sheet. When you are making | 161
several carbon copies and the pack is too bulky to insert easily into | 175
your machine, be sure to use the paper release to get the pack started. | 190
To keep the sheets in a thick pack from slipping, crease a strip of | 203
paper or drop the flap of an envelope over the top edge of the pack | 217
before you start; remove the strip of paper or the envelope after the | 231
pack is inserted. | 234

↓

2 When you are typing on a carbon pack and find that you must | 12 | 246
make an erasure, take a few simple precautions to do the work neatly. | 26 | 260
You will be wise, for example, to hold the carbon pack with one hand | 40 | 274
while you turn up the pack into position for erasing; unless you do | 54 | 288
so, the pack may slip out of alignment. You will also want to keep | 67 | 301
the copies from getting smeared by placing a small card directly | 80 | 314
behind the sheet on which you are erasing; keep moving the card | 93 | 327
back from copy to copy as you work through the pack. To erase on | 106 | 340
carbon copies, use a soft eraser and make sure to keep the eraser | 119 | 353
clean to avoid smearing your work. An ordinary pencil eraser will | 133 | 367
work quite well if you take the trouble to rub it clean on a piece of | 147 | 381
scrap paper before you start. | 153 | 387

PROBLEM 2. Type this letter in the semiblock style. Use Form 3-2.

(74 words in body)

Dr. Samuel R. Westbury   53 East Valley Road   Lawrenceburg, Kentucky 40342 Dear Dr. Westbury: When the Directors meet next week, I must submit the names of those members whose dues for the year are not yet paid in full. The only way I know to get out of that unpleasant assignment is to ask everybody to pay at once. ¶ There is, for example, a balance of $10 outstanding on your dues. Please do both of us a favor by mailing your check for that amount to me today. Cordially yours, **OAKDALE COUNTRY CLUB** Treasurer   HH:

PROBLEM 3. Type the following letter in the semiblock style. Use Form 3-3.

The body of the letter contains all the letters of the alphabet. The large number of capitalized words will also give you practice in shifting.

(231 words in body)

Mr. Vance Bryson, Sports Editor   Louisville Tribune-Sentinel   Kentucky News Building Louisville, Kentucky 40203 Dear **Mr. Bryson:** You will be pleased to hear that you have an impressive list of readers in and around Frankfort. After your column appeared in Saturday's paper, scores of people called me to say that they had read it. ¶ I know that you will be disturbed, however, to hear that your account of the scheduling of the Mid-States Open here at Oakdale is the cause of a serious misunderstanding. Please use your best efforts to erase the false notion that Oakdale Country Club called off the Kentucky Junior Tournament so that we could seize the honor of being host to the Mid-States Open. ¶ The fact is that the Kentucky Junior Tournament has not been canceled. Last week the Country Club of Owensboro very graciously offered the use of its course for that event this year—an offer which was made and accepted before we replied to the bid from Mid-States. ¶ Never was there any thought of requesting the Juniors to change their dates at Oakdale or to seek a different spot. On the contrary, the Direc-

tors of Oakdale voted to recommend that the Club hold to our original agreement. The change was made solely on the initiative of Rex Halpern, Steve Turner, and the other officers of the Juniors, who insisted that we should not miss the once-in-a-lifetime chance to be host to the Mid-States Open.   Sincerely yours, **OAKDALE COUNTRY CLUB**   President **WWL:**

TYPING AN ENCLOSURE NOTATION. An enclosure notation is typed two line spaces below the identifying initials. Type the word *Enclosure* for a single enclosure or the word *Enclosures* and the appropriate number when there is more than one (*Enclosures 3*, for example). Some offices permit the use of the abbreviation *Enc.* or *Encl.*

Provide for the enclosure notation in planning the placement of the letter by raising the starting point one line.

---

letter a check for $25.35 to reimburse you for your expenses.

Cordially yours,

OAKDALE COUNTRY CLUB

Secretary

GLG:XXX

Enclosure

PROBLEM 4. The following letter has an enclosure notation. Type the letter in the semiblock style. Use Form 3-4.

(69 words in body)

Mr. Henry V. Kane, President   Westco Manufacturing Company   450 West Seventh Avenue   Jeffersonville, Indiana 47130 Dear Mr. Kane: Is there any need for me to say that your talk to us on Tuesday evening was a thrilling experience for everyone present? I am sure that you sensed the enthusiasm of your audience even before the ovation at the end. Thank you again for bringing us your inspiring words. ¶ It is a pleasure to enclose with this letter a check for $25.35 to reimburse you for your expenses.   Cordially yours,   **OAKDALE COUNTRY CLUB**   Secretary GLG: Enclosure

Speed Building

Set margin stops for a 60-space line.   Set the line space lever at 1.   Type each line twice (except the paragraph).   Double-space after each two-line group.

WORD DRILL.   The same 3-letter high-frequency combination appears in all words of a line.   Boost your speed by mastering the pattern of each combination.

```
the their theirs them theme then theory there thereby these
which while whine whip whirls whisk whisker whisper whistle
word wore work workman world worm worse worship worst worth
place plaid plain plan plane plank plant plate play playful
marble march margin marine marks market marsh remark marvel
quick quicken quickly quiet quilt quit quite acquit inquire
```

SENTENCE WRITING.   These sentences are meant for speed.   Try to type them at your best rate.   They contain many of the words you have just practiced.

```
Their plan is to march quickly from the marsh to the plain.
Whisper the theory to the workman if he goes there to work.
The world market for their marble may thereby become worse.
These children whistle and play while the workman is there.
The quiet plaid which she wore is not quite worth the cost.
Quite the worst place for them to place the plant is there.
```
———1———2———3———4———5———6———7———8———9———10———11———

PARAGRAPH PREVIEW.   Concentrate on your stroking as you type these words.   Try to type each line more smoothly on the second typing than on the first typing.

```
too carriage squeeze off unless excess sluggishly back over
much oil few times parts typewriter advised serviceman each
```

PARAGRAPH TYPING.   *Move the line space lever to 2.   Set a stop for a 5-space indention.*   Type this paragraph line for line.

Words

```
     Avoid the use of much oil on your typewriter; too much        11
oil may make the machine work sluggishly.  Just squeeze one        23
drop of oil now and then on each end of the guide rails and        35
run the typewriter carriage back and forth a few times over        47
the rails; then be sure to wipe off excess oil.  Do not oil        59
any machine parts unless advised to do so by a serviceman.         71
```
———1———2———3———4———5———6———7———8———9———10———11———

WARM-UP   They wish to spend half of the big profit for an endowment.

ALPHABET   Lazy boys wanted him to adjust five or six square packages.

CONTROL   Eileen took the football to the tall professional fullback.

LETTER PLACEMENT. You have been given detailed directions for the placement of the letters you have so far typed. There is, however, nothing difficult about letter placement.

The placement of a letter depends basically on the number of words in the body of the letter. When the body of the letter is short, you will use a short line and start the letter fairly well down on the sheet. When the body of the letter is long, you will use a longer line and start the letter nearer the top.

The following Letter Placement Guide shows how you can easily plan the placement of letters.

Letter Placement Guide

Words in body	Line length	First line of inside address*
Up to 50	4 inches	25
50 to 75	4 inches	24
75 to 100	4 inches	23
100 to 125	5 inches	22
125 to 150	5 inches	21
150 to 175	5 inches	20
175 to 200	5 inches	19
200 to 225	6 inches	18
225 to 250	6 inches	17
250 and up	6 inches	16

*Lower the starting point one line when the letter is typed on an elite-type machine—but never below line 25.

PROBLEM 1. Type the following letter in the semiblock style. Use Form 3-1.

Follow the Placement Guide. The illustration on this page, in reduced form, shows how this letter looks when typed on a pica-type machine.

The body of the letter contains all the letters of the alphabet.

(84 words in body)

Mr. Leonard J. Mifflin   2963 North Fifth Street   Madison, Wisconsin 53704   Dear Mr. Mifflin: Please note how the placement guide divides letters into just three sizes for purposes of determining the line length. You are told to use a four-inch line when the body of the letter contains fewer than 100 words, a five-inch line when the number of words is between 100 and 200, and a six-inch line when the word count goes over 200. ¶ This plan, which takes only a moment to learn, meets the highest requirements of business for good letter placement.   Cordially yours,   OAKDALE COUNTRY CLUB   Managing Director   WSR:

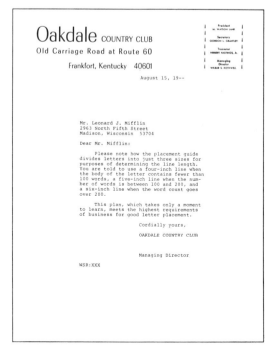

Line length for this page—60 spaces. Set margin stops. Set the line space lever at 2. Set a stop for a 5-space indention. These paragraphs have been devised for maximum speed. Make your fingers fly! Omit the numbers when you type the paragraphs.

Words

1

The busy ant is known for the work it does and for the   11
social tendencies it displays; it is an authentic marvel of   23
the insect world. When there is work to do, the ant is not   35
idle; it goes to work with downright vigor and such visible   47
proficiency that men envy it, and it is also quick to go to   59
the aid of others with more work than they can handle.   70
——1——2——3——4——5——6——7——8——9——10——11——

2

An element of risk goes with driving an auto under the   11   81
usual conditions, when big signs and signals aid the driver   23   93
to make the right stops and turns. When fog hangs over the   35 105
road so that such signs and signals become visible just for   47 117
short distances, the risk is then so big that men and women   59 129
then driving make the right choice if they decide to halt.   71 141
——1——2——3——4——5——6——7——8——9——10——11——

3

Ancient man did not know that he could find fuel if he   11 152
dug down into the ground for it; the history of coal and of   23 164
the other fuels men burn today spans centuries, but it does   35 176
not form any big part of world history. Fuel is the key to   47 188
power; the giant industrial firms of this land and of other   59 200
lands did not begin until coal came into use for fuel.   70 211
——1——2——3——4——5——6——7——8——9——10——11——

4

Fish form part of the usual diet of most men and women   11 222
of this land and of other lands around the world; authentic   23 234
studies of ancient man lead us to the firm belief that fish   35 246
also formed part of his diet. Such studies may entitle the   47 258
fish to the title of the most ancient element of human diet   59 270
and make it an aid to man for more time than any other item   71 282
of diet. The quantity of edible fish used today is big, so   83 294
that corps of men prowl the oceans for fish and bring their   95 306
hauls to the docks of the town or city for sale. Such work 107 318
may make some men rich, but it is also work that may embody 119 330
big risks; if days of work fail to land any big quantity of 131 342
fish, the fish sold may not pay for the cost of the work. 142 353
——1——2——3——4——5——6——7——8——9——10——11——

WELLS
SHOE COMPANY
1684 North Colonial Street
Worcester, Massachusetts 01608

February 16, 19--

Mr. Gerald D. Morrison
930 West Keller Street
Buffalo, New York 14221

Dear Mr. Morrison:

The semiblock style in which this letter is typed is a style that is widely used in business. It is, in general, the same style you have already learned. Four parts, however, have been added--the inside address, the company name, the dictator's title, and the initials that identify the dictator and the typist.

The position of the date depends upon office preference. A semiblock letter may have the date centered, typed to end with the right margin, or located as it is here.

When you use office stationery, type the date two line spaces below the letterhead. Since most business letterheads are two inches deep, the date will usually be typed on the fourteenth line.

Start all lines of the inside address at the left margin. Leave one line space before the salutation and one line space after the complimentary close. Type the dictator's title four lines down from the company name.

Sincerely yours,

WELLS SHOE COMPANY

Sales Manager

JWM:XXX

Model Letter 2—Semiblock Style Business Letter
Mixed Punctuation

Line length: 5 inches	Words in body: 153
Date: Line 14	Inside address starts: Line 20

method — Count strokes ÷ by 2 center — then backspace that no.

LESSON 20

Centering

The appearance of typed material is always improved by proper placement. This lesson provides the basic principles for centering headings and for centering material on the page. You will also get training and practice in the practical application of those principles.

HORIZONTAL CENTERING. The quickest and easiest way to center a title or a heading horizontally is to use the backspace key. Just follow these steps after you have inserted the paper.

1. Clear all margin and tabulator stops.

2. Locate the printing point at the center of the sheet.

3. Backspace once for every two stroke spaces in the title or heading.

4. Start to type when you have finished backspacing.

The key to accurate work is making sure that you backspace from the center of the sheet.

When the left edge of the paper is at 0 on the line scale, the center of a standard 8½ by 11 sheet is at 42 if your machine has pica type and at 51 if your machine has elite type.

A good way to prevent confusion in your backspacing is to depress the backspace key for one stroke in the heading and release it for the next stroke. *2 strokes one backsp.*

Study this example.

AN EASY PLAN

Depress for A
Release for N

Depress for *space*
Release for E

Depress for A
Release for S

Depress for Y
Release for *space*

Depress for P
Release for L

Depress for A
Release for N

You may find it helpful to say each letter or space to yourself as you depress or release the backspace key.

Note. One advantage of this method is that you can use it on all makes and all models of typewriters. You should, however, examine your own machine to see whether it is equipped with any special devices to help you in centering. Some Underwood models, for example, have a dual scale on the front of the machine to enable you to center a heading without backspacing.

PROBLEM 1. Use a half sheet of paper (8½ inches wide) for this problem.

Set the line space regulator for double spacing. Because everything is to be typed in capital letters, you should also depress the shift lock to eliminate shifting for each letter.

Space down three double spaces from the top edge and center this heading.

AN EASY PLAN

Next, space down two double spaces and type the following heading.

Note. When a heading contains an uneven number of stroke spaces, disregard the left-over stroke. In this line, for example, do not backspace for the letter *S* in HEADINGS.

FOR TYPING HEADINGS

Space down two double spaces and type this line.

IN THE CENTER OF

Finally, space down two double spaces and type this fourth line.

A STANDARD SHEET OF PAPER

VERTICAL CENTERING. As you learned early in your course, there are six typewriter lines to a vertical inch. The depth of a standard 8½ by 11 sheet of paper is thus 66 lines (6 x 11 = 66).

To center typed material vertically on the sheet, (1) find the number of lines that you will need, (2) subtract that number from 66, and (3) divide by 2. The figure you get is the line number on which to start typing.

The lines you will need include, of course, both typed lines *and* blank lines (referred to as interlines).

WARM-UP   It is the duty of the chairman to work with vigor for them.

ALPHABET   Alf expected both wives to make an amazingly quiet journey.

CONTROL   Nell sells tennis balls and rubber balloons for her school.

PROBLEM 1. Study Model Letter 2 on the next page; then type it on the letterhead in your Workbook (Form 2-1).

Use today's date and your own initials on all letters. Double-space after the dictator's title; then type the initials at the left margin.

PROBLEM 2. Read the following letter carefully; then type it in the semiblock style. Use a 5-inch line. Start the inside address on line 19. Use Form 2-2.

The punctuation of a well-planned business letter follows a definite pattern. Most business offices designate the exact style that is to be used to punctuate all letters. Today one style that is extensively used is the *mixed punctuation* style explained in the body of the following letter. The content of this letter, therefore, is an important part of your course.

The body of the letter contains all the letters of the alphabet.

(*186 words in body*)

Wallace & Anderson, Inc.   2638 Pioneer Boulevard   Oakland, California 94604 Gentlemen: The style of punctuation that you are now using is referred to as "mixed punctuation." Disregarding the body of the letter, the only lines that have end punctuation are the salutation and the complimentary close. There are no marks after the date, the lines of the inside address, the company name, or the dictator's title. ¶ You realize, of course, that an abbreviation requires a period regardless of the way the letter is punctuated. Be sure to type that period even though the abbreviation does come at the end of a line. ¶ The colon is the only punctuation mark that you should use after the salutation of a typed letter. Do not use a dash or a hyphen. Although you will sometimes see a comma used in place of the colon, the comma is generally considered correct only when the letter is a penwritten note to a close friend. ¶ No mark other than the comma is ever used, on the other hand, after the complimentary close. The comma after the complimentary close is just as correct for a business letter as it is for a personal letter.   Very truly yours,   **WELLS SHOE COMPANY** Treasurer   BFL:

PROBLEM 3. Type the following letter in the semiblock style. Use a 5-inch line. Start the inside address on line 22. Use Form 2-3.

The body of the letter contains all the letters of the alphabet and all the figures.

(*111 words in body*)

H. H. Darlington and Sons, Inc.   Broad Street at Third Avenue   Chattanooga, Tennessee 37401   Gentlemen: Thank you for your Purchase Order No. 6302-J. Your order is being filled at once. You will surely get delivery within the next few days—in plenty of time for your scheduled sale. ¶ We are taking the liberty of making one change that we feel sure you will approve. ¶ The moccasin-type men's lounge slipper listed on your order—Style No. 471—is now available only in broken sizes. Because we know that you want a properly balanced stock for your sale, we are filling that part of your order with Style No. 958. There is a slight difference in design, but there is no difference in quality or in price.   Sincerely yours, **WELLS SHOE COMPANY**   Office Manager KLP:

Look at the FOREWORD reproduced below. Note the extra interline under the heading.

FOREWORD

The author of a manuscript sometimes
prefers to include a short foreword or a
preface. Such material should be placed
on a separate page and carefully centered
to give it a pleasing appearance and to
set it off from the body of the work.

The space occupied by this FOREWORD is 14 lines.

Heading............................	1
Interlines below heading..............	2
Typed lines in body..................	6
Interlines in body....................	5
	14

The total remaining space on the sheet is thus 66 — 14, or 52 lines. When you divide by 2 (for the two margins), you get 26. To center this FOREWORD vertically on an 8½ by 11 sheet, type the heading on line 26.

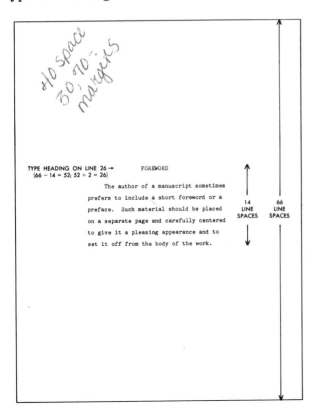

Note. Centered material looks best when the bottom margin is slightly deeper than the top margin. The plan that you are learning here provides automatically for such placement. By typing the heading on line 26, for example, you will have a top margin of 25 lines and a bottom margin of 27 lines.

The FOREWORD you have been studying was typed to a 40-space line. The same FOREWORD—typed this time to a 48-space line—is pictured below. Note that there are now five lines in the body, instead of six lines.

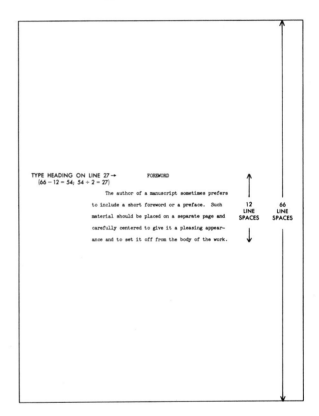

The correct line for *this* heading, you'll notice, is line 27.

PROBLEM 2. Type on an 8½ by 11 sheet of paper the FOREWORD shown at the top of this page.

If your machine has pica type, use a 40-space line. If your machine has elite type, use a 48-space line.

Set margin stops for the correct line length. Set a tabulator stop for a 5-space paragraph indention.

Double-space the body of your work. Triple-space after the heading.

October 15, 19--

Dear Harriet:

The style in which this letter is typed is a
good style to use in typing letters to your friends.
There are, you will notice, just four parts to the
letter--the date, the salutation, the body, and the
complimentary close.

Note that the date and the complimentary close
start at the center. This position for the date is
more convenient than other acceptable locations.

The salutation always starts at the left margin.
Its position vertically on the sheet depends on the
length of your letter. Double-space after the salutation.

Most letters are now typed with single spacing,
with double spacing between paragraphs. Double-space
after the last paragraph--before you type the complimentary close.

You should set two tabulator stops. Use one
stop for a five-space paragraph indention. Set the
other stop at the center of the sheet for the start
of the date and of the complimentary close.

Cordially yours,

Model Letter 1—Personal Letter (Semiblock Style)

Line length: 5 inches

Date: Line 14   Salutation: Line 20

Note: The model letters in this book are slightly reduced reproduc-
tions of letters that were originally typed in pica type. The line length—
given in inches—is also correct for elite type. When the letter is typed
on an elite machine, it will have more spaces to the line—and thus fewer
lines—than the model. Drop the starting point of a letter one line for
elite type. Type the salutation of this letter, for example, on line 21 if
you are using an elite machine.

SELECTING THE LINE LENGTH. The size of the article that you are centering on an 8½ by 11 sheet determines the line length that you will use. This Guide will help you to select the best line length.

Centering Guide

Number of Strokes	Line Length
Up to 500	4 inches
500 to 1,000	5 inches
Over 1,000	6 inches

ESTIMATING STROKES. Unless the material you are typing is quite short, you will waste time by making an actual count of the strokes. Simply count the strokes in any average line, multiply that count by the number of full lines, and add the number of strokes in any short lines.

Be sure to count the spaces between words and the spaces after punctuation marks.

ESTIMATING THE NUMBER OF LINES. After you get the estimated number of strokes, you will know the line length to which you will do your typing. To get the number of typed lines, simply divide the total number of strokes by the number of strokes in each line.

Assume, for example, that you estimate the number of strokes in the article shown below to be 868. You will use a 5-inch line. The number of typed lines, therefore, will be 868 ÷ 50, or 17+ (18), if you have a pica-type machine. If your machine has elite type, the number of typed lines will be 868 ÷ 60, or 14+ (15). Unless the division is even, use the next higher number.

That number does not, of course, include the interlines or the heading. Remember to include them in planning vertical placement.

PROBLEM 3. Type the following article with double spacing on an 8½ by 11 sheet of paper. Triple-space below the heading. Set a tabulator stop for a 5-space paragraph indention.

Read through the article first. It contains suggestions to help you in converting inches into stroke spaces.

This article contains all the letters of the alphabet.

INCHES TO SPACES

For the typing of manuscripts and letters, it is often more convenient to establish a line length in terms of inches rather than in terms of spaces. In order to set margin stops properly, however, you need to know how many spaces there are in the line length you select.

To convert inches to spaces, just remember that each inch of pica type contains 10 spaces and that each inch of elite type contains 12 spaces. If you select a 5-inch line for your work, therefore, the line length is 50 pica spaces or 60 elite spaces.

A sheet of paper of standard size is exactly 8½ inches wide. There are thus 85 available pica spaces or 102 available elite spaces. You can get quickly the total number of spaces in both margins by subtracting the number of spaces in the line from the number of available spaces. To find the spaces in either margin, divide that figure by 2.

Using Your Typing Skill

In this section of your typing course you will learn to type personal and business letters. You will also get training in typing on cards and envelopes, in arranging tabulations, in preparing outlines, themes, and manuscripts, and in making many other practical applications of typing skill.

Each Practice Unit starts with three drill sentences. Those sentences have been carefully devised to help you improve your stroking.

The first sentence is always a fast warm-up sentence. All the words in it are balanced-hand words. The second sentence contains all the letters of the alphabet. The third line—a control sentence—stresses either capitals, double letters, or figures.

Start your work with each unit by typing the sentences on a half sheet of paper.

Set the left margin stop for a 60-space line and push the other stop out of the way to keep the bell from ringing. Set the line space lever at 1. Space down seven lines from the top edge of the sheet.

Follow this practice schedule.

1. Type the Warm-up sentence three times with single spacing. *Try for top speed.* Double-space after the 3-line group.

2. Type the Alphabet and Control sentences three times each with single spacing. Double-space after each 3-line group. *Try for absolute accuracy.*

3. Check your typing of the Alphabet and Control sentences for accuracy. If you made an error in typing either sentence, type that sentence two more times.

Practice Unit 1	Learning Basic Letter Form

WARM UP   Bid for an authentic antique ivory ornament for the chapel.

ALPHABET   He may now have quit making black jars for pure zinc oxide.

CONTROL   Sidney sailed from Cleveland to Duluth via the Great Lakes.

PROBLEM 1. Study Model Letter 1 on the next page. The body of the letter contains important instructions.

After you have made a thorough study of Model Letter 1, type the letter on a sheet of plain paper. Use today's date instead of the date shown.

PROBLEM 2. Type the following letter on a sheet of plain paper in the exact form of Model Letter 1. Place the letter in the same position as the Model Letter. Date it today. *This letter contains all the letters of the alphabet.*

¶ indicates the start of a new paragraph.

Dear Gerald: **Like so many other inventions, the typewriter is one of the great work-savers of our age. Anyone who takes the trouble to learn to type finds that he can dispose of his correspondence in a fraction of the** time needed to do the same job by hand. ¶ **Men and women in every occupation and in every walk of life are now typists. They utilize their skill to write letters and reports, to do club work, to care for personal affairs, and to expedite all kinds of business. ¶ In the days when typewriters were rarely found outside the business office, some people felt that a typed letter lacked the "personal touch" of a note written by hand. That idea has now almost entirely disappeared. ¶ Most people today definitely prefer to receive typewritten letters because such letters are quickly read. A typed letter properly placed on the sheet is far more pleasing to the eye than the scratches that most of us make when we write by hand. Sincerely yours,**